The Art of Living

Falstaff, the Fool, and Dino

STARR GOODE

ACACIA BOOKS PRESS

Selections from the *The Art of Living* have been published as:

"Falstaff and the Art of Living." *New Laurel Review*, Volume XXV, 2012.

"Falstaff and the Art of Living." *Green Hills Literary Lantern*, XXII, 2011, Truman State University.

"In Praise of the Fool." *Westview*, Fall/Winter 2013, Volume 30, Number 1, a journal of Western Oklahoma, Southwestern Oklahoma State University.

"In Praise of the Fool." *Word River Literary Review*, Spring 2012, University of Nevada.

"Dino and the Art of Livin' Good," in an upcoming edition of in *Cantaraville*, a literary quarterly.

Cover images:

Ralph Richardson as Falstaff in a 1945 Old Vic production of *Henry IV Parts One and Two*. Considered the greatest Falstaff in living memory. *Granger, NYC—All rights reserved*.

Portrait of the wily Court Jester Gonella from Ferrara, Italy by Jean Fouquet, 1445. *Wikimedia Commons/Public Domain*.

Dean Martin, studio publicity photo for the film, *The Bells Are Ringing*, 1960. *Wikimedia Commons/Public Domain*.

To Charles Sherman
For his lightness of spirit

Prologue

The Art of Living

Past an open door, I saw some orange nasturtiums growing among the stones. Beyond that, the labyrinth lay out in our hostess's backyard. On this late summer afternoon, a group of friends had come to walk it. One by one we entered, moved round in circles trying to get to the center. Just as I approached that center, the path would turn back on itself and take me out to the circumference. Overhead, the sky provided a rare cover of clouds, the effects of Hurricane Dennis, and, beneath my feet, I felt the resilient grass. For a brief moment, I had the sensation of existing in several worlds all at once.

One year earlier on another August day, I had walked a labyrinth in Forest Lawn, yes, that Forest Lawn, so darkly rendered in Evelyn Waugh's satire *The Loved One*. A monument to some of the worst excesses of Southern California culture—but there is an unexpected treasure to be found nestled in those dry hills. On the forecourt of the "Gardens of Contemplation," is a beautiful stone labyrinth modeled after the one at Chartres Cathedral in France. All about the grounds, scattered groups of people were laying flowers down, attending to the dead. And so was I. My women's circle had brought me here just days after my father's funeral.

In both labyrinths, when I finally did reach the center, I paused. A pleasurable permission to do nothing but stand still and take a breath. At Forest Lawn, came a flood of gratitude that I am still alive. At the other, a comforting thought: "In a labyrinth, no matter how lost you feel, you're always headed towards the center." Then driving home, north on the 405, a freeway I've driven a thousand times, the realization that I was going the wrong way punctured my dreamy state of mind. After an initial panic of *where am I?*"—it took a little while to reorient myself and change directions. Once back at my house, I rested upon a blue daybed, thinking about the weeks to come; I should be preparing for classes, the summer's almost over. To counter all this, I turned on the radio and drifted into a delicious nap.

After an hour or so, sounds from the airwaves, a broadcast of human voices began to wake me. A woman and a man are talking about the "serious matter of play—we are not human without it." The man, director of the National Institute for Play, describes our biological design as hardwired for a lifetime of play. Without pleasurable, purposeless activity, we lose our capacity for joy. Without spontaneous eruptions of play, we become rigid, depressed, and have no sense of wit. We become efficient at doing our duty and enduring life. How many of us seek the company of young children because they allow us to return to the vitalizing, timeless state of play?

Part of our cultural heritage is this devotion to work, the Protestant ethic which is the enemy of play. Growing up, I don't remember anyone talking about joy. And now as an adult, I wonder about how do we get back to ourselves, to that lost center? I raise such questions with my beloved uncle, my mother's brother, the oldest surviving member of the family. My uncle tells me this topic is the most significant one that humans face—what virtues should a person cultivate in order to live a happy life?

Falstaff

The "most completely good man in all of drama" says Orson Welles of Falstaff

The Art of Living

I like to get up when I want, when I feel like it. As a child, I'd set my clock late, to the last possible minute. I regarded school as a severe limitation on my freedom, even at times, a prison. At ten, I remember looking out the window of my fifth grade classroom; in the distance, I saw the high school building. An oppressive gravity pulled my spirit down, "When I finish here, I'm going to have to put in four years over there." As an adult, I have done all I can to avoid work which would force me to get up according to someone else's idea of time.

This is why I love Falstaff, why I loved him from his first words exchanged with Prince Henry (also known as Hal or Harry) in Shakespeare's *Henry IV* histories. These plays, set in early 15th century England, chronicle the civil war King Henry IV plunged the country into after his murder of Richard II.

King Henry IV

Sir John Falstaff

The prince becomes Henry V when his father dies at the end of the second play. For me, the most important aspect of the *Henriad* is not the royalty or their wars, but the chance to meet Falstaff! Regardless of the outer circumstances he faces–poverty, the threat of arrest, war, Falstaff maintains an inner equanimity. Like any great sage, he feels free to enjoy the blessing of life. In his very first line of dialogue, he asks the prince, "Now Hal, what time of day is it, lad?" And the prince who knows him well replies: "What a devil hast thou to do with the time of day?" For Falstaff is the master of his own time, that is to say, of his own life. Actually, his freedom lies in the fact that he has no idea what time it is. When what you devote your life to is roasted capons, Spanish wine, and bawdy women, but most of all, to the power of your own wit–what *has* the time of day to do with you?

His joyful spirit seems to me to be just the antidote to these barren times of overwork in jobs that afford little meaning and to an increasing oppression by the machine of state. Falstaff possesses an overflowing exuberance about his own existence. He thieves by night, sponges off the prince, well, really off anybody he can, especially Mistress Quickly, proprietress of his favorite tavern in Eastcheap. Glutton, drunk, debauch, what are the Seven Deadly Sins to this Lord of Play? Falstaff constructs his own morality, believes in his right to live as he wants.

Mistress Quickly and Falstaff

When informed by Prince Hal that he must command a brigade of soldiers in the ongoing civil war, the fat knight responds with a practical intelligence: "Hostess, my breakfast; come!"

Falstaff and Doll Tearsheet

Those he uses come back for more, drawn by the magnetism of his life force. Let us dispense with any dreary analysis of the merry crowd at the Boar's Head Tavern as co-dependent enablers, affixed to a sociopath. Falstaff can't be explained by technical jargon—his energy bursts beyond the bounds of categories. If Mistress Quickly in a rare fit of pique tries to have him arrested because for decades, "He hath eaten me out of house and home," she soon realizes she has never known "an honester and truer-hearted man."

Falstaff arrested at the suit of Mistress Quickly

Falstaff persuades Mistress Quickly not only to drop her lawsuit but to lend him more money!

He *is* true, true to himself, true to his deepest value—the playful expression of his wit. One of his grandest stories is the tale of how last midnight on a highway near Gadshill, he held up some pilgrims on the road to Canterbury.

At the Boar's Head Tavern,
Falstaff tells the tale of his attack by 50 thieves

Then, in turn, he was attacked by a mob of thieves and had to fight "with fifty of them." Prince Hal, however, catches his friend in faults of logic. Everyone knows the story is a big fat lie, especially the prince as he was one of the *two* masked men who robbed Falstaff as a prank.

Hal and Poins (2 men!) wearing masks, rout Falstaff and his cohorts

But that's not the point! It's not about literal truth but soaring metaphor made into myth. As an artist, Falstaff takes all the time he needs to entertain the crowd around the tavern's fire. But when the prince tries to pierce his story with the prick of reason, with demands for consistency, Falstaff refuses to be commanded to explain himself: "What, upon compulsion?" Even, he says, if he were being tortured on "all the racks in the world, I would not tell you on compulsion." Oh, to be as strong and self-composed as Falstaff in the face of a hectoring bully. Not even the prince, heir to the throne, can force him to act against himself.

For Falstaff likes himself, and unlike the prince, is capable of love. He takes relish in the experience of being alive. Perhaps this magnanimous nature is why I can forgive

Falstaff everything and Henry nothing. From the prince's first soliloquy, we can see that he has already gone over to the dark side, secretly allied himself to the royal forces of power and greed. He lies to his friends with menace and icy calculation to ensure his ascent to the throne. Falstaff creates for the joy of it. Then again maybe I shouldn't be too hard on Hal when one considers his family. What could one expect from him with that butcher of a father, Henry IV, who usurped the throne and set all of England aflame in civil war.

Henry of Bolingbroke claims the throne in 1399

And that monster of a brother, Prince John, who swore by the honor of his blood to give amnesty to the rebel nobles, then without hesitating, executed them all. Such is the inheritance of Prince Henry.

Chilled by the spectacle of Prince John's misdeed, Falstaff pronounces his worst condemnation of him: a man who cannot be made to laugh. He then reflects on Prince Henry's poor genetic line, on "the cold blood he did naturally inherit of his father." Cold indeed. Falstaff feels he has done the young prince a world of good by introducing him to the healing properties of his favorite drink, the Spanish wine, sherry-sack. In Falstaff's charming soliloquy on the sanguine influences of drinking sack, he exults how it warms the blood, fires the imagination, and gives the heart courage: "Hereof comes it that Prince Harry is valiant." And Falstaff gives us his thoughts on parental duty: "If I had a thousand sons, the first humane principle I would teach them should be,... to addict themselves to sack." Lucky for the prince to have an older friend like Jack Falstaff who views the world in such a completely different way than that grim royal family. Or at least that's how the old knight sees it.

But often the play is viewed by critics as the story of a young man growing up—casting off the sins of his youth, to take up his manly responsibilities. I reject this analysis; the prince never changes! From the first, he only pretends to be "base" so that when he reveals his true kingly essence, it will appear all the more glorious. The prince does not transform from a state of dissolution to one of maturity. Mature to do what–become the biggest war monger on the continent? Let us not forget, his first act as king, as Henry V, is to invade France and renew the Hundred Years War. This fatal aggression confirms that he has cunningly followed his father's deathbed advice:

> Be it thy course to busy giddy minds
> With foreign quarrels....

An old but still effective political trick–distract the populace from civil unrest by unifying them with the threat of a foreign enemy. It seems so clear to me that the moral of the plays is not about how young Hal learns to become a wise king by shedding off those disreputable characters of Eastcheap, but how he betrays the vital qualities of life embodied by Falstaff. Hardly a model of leadership, he becomes a killer, a warrior-king bent on expanding his territory through military power.

If, in the meantime, he loses his resolve and lingers in the pleasures of Falstaff's company, who can blame him? He knows the terrible burden of his dying father's ambition and is drawn to Falstaff's vitality, his freedom to be himself. To be fair, young Hal has some wit himself, or he couldn't find Falstaff so attractive. And Falstaff couldn't take such delight in their conversations, couldn't comment on the prince's "unsavory similes," or be inspired to "keep Prince Harry in continual laughter" with tales of his misadventures. But who really is there in that world to understand Falstaff? The old man mistakenly thinks it is the prince.

He loves Harry as a son. It is the one way that Falstaff is not free–he has a heart. He calls out frequently for love from Hal: "[A]nd thou lovest me," "if thou lovest me," "thy love is worth a million." Never do such words escape from the prince's lips. Strange to say perhaps, that the chaotic Falstaff has something to teach the prince about how to live, but he does. There is much fun and sport available to the lads at the Boar's Head Tavern with their companionable drinking, wild stories, play-acting. One evening, Falstaff takes on the role of Prince Henry and as him, pleads his case for the rightness of their relationship. Falstaff strongly defends his qualities: is it a sin to be "old and merry"? The king may have cause to banish others from his son's company but he must *never, never* do so to "sweet Jack Falstaff, kind Jack Falstaff, true Jack Falstaff, valiant Jack Falstaff." To banish the protean Falstaff would be as immense as to "banish all the world."

Even so, the prince, in his role as the king, replies with coldness, "I do, I will." The old knight can only hope this rejection is still part of the pretense of their play. But Hal's unforgivable malice cannot be disguised when he sends Falstaff to war on foot. The prince amuses himself with the image of the fat Sir Jack fatally collapsing from the exertion of marching a few hundred yards. But the irrepressible Falstaff has his own way of preparing for war. Whereas the king calls for "never-dying honor" and whereas young Henry vows to wash away his past shame with the blood of the rebel Hotspur (some call this taking on mature responsibility) and whereas Hotspur, eager to kill the prince, cries out before the battle: "Doomsday is near; die all, die merrily," Falstaff has one concern and one concern only which is to "fill me a bottle of sack." And, of course, he doesn't pay for it.

Nothing reveals the greatness of Falstaff's character more than his thoughts and actions during the climatic Battle of Shrewsbury. While rebel and royal forces clash in deadly combat, Falstaff remains a whole human being. He can, with tenderness, tell the prince, "I would 'twere bed-time, Hal, and all well." How these few words do puncture all that inflated worship of hot revenge, heroics, glory, honor. He knows that this war is being fought for the betterment of nothing, for a meaningless exchange of political power, a useless waste of life. When he falls down on the bloody field and pretends to be dead in order to escape certain slaughter at the hands of the defiant Earl of Douglas, Falstaff serves life. He then famously resurrects himself and muses, "The better part of valour is discretion; in the which better part, I have saved my life."

Often scholarly pundits cite this incident as proof of Falstaff's cowardice. Nothing could be further from the truth! Falstaff is in full possession of his faculties when he decides with a droll wit to "counterfeit" death; he shows no trace of terror. It is not fear of death that motivates him but a love of life. One of the earliest defenders of Falstaff, critic Maurice Morgann, despite universal opinion to the contrary, declares that Falstaff's courage "was manifest in the conduct and practice of his whole life." His controversial essay written centuries ago in 1777, argues that Falstaff has a natural courage that is "independent of opinion." It is a kind of courage that does not conform to "prevailing modes of honour, and the fashions of the age."

Samuel Phelps, 1845   Henry Beerbohm Tree, 1896   JH Hackett, 1850

The acquisition of honor runs as a thematic thread in the *Henry* plays through the dreary court scenes and the broodings over the king's honor, Harry's honor, Hotspur's honor. Their notions of honor cause the tremendous, violent suffering of war. Shakespeare gives us only one heavy counterweight to all of this–the *mind* of Falstaff. He alone has the courage to stand against the entire culture and its values. By Falstaff's reckoning, honor serves neither the living nor the dead. It can give no relief to the wounded, and nothing can help the dead. Honor is like a scutcheon, a coat of arms to decorate the coffins of the dead–it is of no use. Alone on the stage, he delivers his damning disquisition on honor:

> [H]onor pricks me on. Yea, but how now if honor
> pricks me off when I come on? How then? Can
> honour set to a leg? No. Or an arm? No. Or take
> away the grief of a wound? No. Honour hath
> no skill in surgery then? No. What is honour?

A word. What is in that word, honour? Air. A trim reckoning! Who hath it? He that died o' Wednesday. Doth he feel it? No. Doth he hear it? No. It is insensible then? Yea, to the dead. But will it not live with the living? No. Why? Detraction will not suffer it. Therefore I'll none of it: honour is a mere scutcheon; and so ends my catechism.

Roger Allam as Falstaff wins an Olivier award, 2010

Through Falstaff's words, Shakespeare deflates two millennia of literary tradition, that began with Homer in the *Iliad*; the hero-soldier slaughters his enemies for the glory of an immortal name, an honor often cemented by then dying himself in combat. Thus when the battle starts, the prince desires only to prove himself as a man, a man who can kill in order to attain honor; he also bids Falstaff to say his prayers because "thou owest God a death."

Achilles kills a Trojan prisoner, 4th c. BCE

Slain by Prince Hal, the fallen Hotspur is mourned by his comrades

Falstaff, carrying the corpse of Hotspur, claims to have killed him in battle and gleefully demands a reward: "I look to be either earl or duke"

But Falstaff refuses to give up his life for an abstraction.

How I wish I could say that this warrior's ethos linking brutality to honor has been put to rest, this exultation of life destroying life, but clearly, it is not so. A brief look at popular culture confirms this. Ten minutes in almost any movie theater watching the preview trailers will give you a clear picture of the themes of our culture—violence, more violence, fear, death by guns, death by fiery explosions. Witness the new release of Halo 3 video war games (tested by the military) which had the highest grossing opening day in entertainment history. I read that mingled in the crowds waiting to buy the game were army recruiters as this was their perfect target audience.

Recently I saw the new film *3:10 to Yuma*, a good film with a great actor (Russell Crowe!), a witty, intelligent script, beautiful cinematography, all the grandeur and sweep of the southwest. The whole moral weight of the film leads inexorably to its climax: a man chooses to die, to leave behind a wife and two sons to prove he is honorable. He decides it's better that he should die in a shoot-out as a lesson in honor to his teenage son. Better than being with his boy? Seeing him grow up, taking pleasure with his family, looking into his son's face, holding his wife, working his land? Maimed as a soldier in the Civil War, this impoverished rancher hates his life. One can get caught up in the man's decision—he has no choice, it's the right thing to do, he wants respect. As I sat in the dark in the theater, I found myself falling under the seductive spell of the film, but when the thief (whom the rancher is trying to take to justice), wants to rescue the poor man's life from a useless sacrifice, he quotes Falstaff, "The better part of valor is discretion." That's when I woke up! It's the same old bill of goods being sold, the lone hero who saves civilization through violence. The only lone hero I can think of is Falstaff who saves himself and the rest of us by refusing to be enthralled by death; he saves us all by choosing to live.

It is encouraging, however, to hear the words of the liberating spirit of Falstaff being spoken in a mass market movie—that he is at least *part* of the current zeitgeist. On a smaller scale, a few weeks back, I experienced another tribute to Falstaff while attending a new play, *Clay*, at the prestigious Center Theatre Group's Kirk Douglas Theatre here in Los Angeles. It's the story of a nerdy Jewish kid who is rescued from his miserable life in the suburbs by an older mentor through their mutual love of music.

And just what new form does our age give Falstaff? An African-American hip-hop artist named Sir John who lives in Flatbush. A master rapper, a wordsmith of the highest order, the older black man transforms the white boy Clifford into the self-expressive performer Clay. At least in this play, the young man rejects his toxic father and chooses the tonic Sir John and the path of artistic freedom.

One last word on popular culture. I must say I picked up with dread the last Harry Potter book.

I didn't want Harry to die but an equal anxiety was: does Harry have to turn into a killer? For at least the last two books, Harry's mentor, the supposedly benign wizard Dumbledore, has been telling him he's "got to kill" the evil Lord Voldemort. There can't be any other way. This means that only Harry, today's most famous incarnation of the lone hero, can save the magical world and the ordinary world the rest of us muggles are stuck in.

Harry too believes he is the Chosen One, "It's got to be me." But at the final battle of Hogwarts, Harry as a hero does something different—he shows mercy. He offers Voldemort the chance to repent his evil deeds, to salvage his soul. *And* he doesn't try to kill his enemy but just to disarm him. Voldemort dies by his own hand when the green light of his own killing curse fatally rebounds on him. What a relief that our Harry doesn't have to maim his soul by becoming a murderer. Bless him!

My encounter with Falstaff has been a boon for me. To play is one of life's great enhancements. A hundred years ago, the English critic, A. C. Bradley, named the essence of Falstaff: "The bliss of freedom gained in humour." Everything he does, he does "with the gaiety of a boy."

Antony Sher as Falstaff, 2014

Falstaff's astonishing vitality remains undimmed by age or circumstance. He answers to no law other than the creative urge to express his wit. Renouncing the tyranny of repressive social codes, his joy is to be himself.

In our time of declining empire, would that every child on the Fourth of July be required, no, required is the wrong word when writing of Falstaff, would that every child be *allowed* the opportunity of reading Falstaff's words on honor instead of the usual exhibitions of nostalgia for military glories. May his speech be on the wall of every army recruiting station should some young man or woman be beguiled by empty promises of honor. Let them be beguiled by Falstaff's wit. And please, god of mercy, no more romanticizing of Hal's oft-quoted St. Crispian's Day speech in *Henry V*. Never am I more dry-eyed than when I hear his words to rally the English troops outnumbered by the French on the eve of the Battle of Agincourt:

> If we are marked to die, we are enough
> to do our country loss; and if to live,
> The fewer men, the greater share of honour.

King Henry V at the Battle of Agincourt, 1415

I remember sitting in the front row at a production of *Henry V*, watching the action unfold as the English ministers and clergy came up with the flimsiest of legal pretenses to invade France. Then as the Battle of Agincourt progressed, as I sat with red Jell-O "blood" spilling over from the stage onto my clothes, I had one sure thought—this battle is for nothing. History bears me out—in a few short years, the French (Joan of Arc led the charge!) drove the English out.

Joan of Arc

And yet, only yesterday I heard on the radio an NPR report about an executive-training seminar called Movers and Shakespeare meeting in Aspen, Colorado to study Henry V for his leadership skills. Further research on this led me to a *Washington Post* article about a witty debate held in 2004 with Washington insiders and media pundits, on whether Henry V was right or wrong to invade France (with much comparison to the current war in Iraq). At the end of the argument, Dame Judi Dench, the renowned British actress was asked to judge who won. Her response was to read the last lines of the play which point to the complete futility of the war as the young Henry VI and his counselors straight-away "lost France and made his England bleed."

The last word belongs to Falstaff. Only he can reveal in an indelible moment of humanity all we really need to know about war. Falstaff, surveying the carnage of battle, says, "Give me life."

Orson Welles as Falstaff, 1965

The Art of Living

The Fool

The Fool Tarot card, Rider-Waite-Smith deck, 1909

One languid Sunday afternoon as I lay on my bed, I felt via the electromagnetism of the radio waves, the voice of Nina Simone wash through me and fill the room with yearning:

I wish I knew how it would feel to be free,
I wish I could break all the chains holding me.

I wanted to feel free too! Decades ago back in Berkeley, amidst the study of many things which were part of the spirit of those heady times, I developed a passion for a system of symbols known as the Tarot. The cards begin not with the number one but with a zero above an image titled the Fool. How strange, I thought, to begin before the beginning. In Western Mystery schools, the tarot cards are studied in sequence to gain insight about the journey of human consciousness. The quality of mind necessary to move from intention to completion in any cycle of manifestation is shown in the image of the Fool. And just what quintessential quality does the Fool represent? It is a sense of freedom.

Tarot cards have an ancient yet obscure origin; some say an Egyptian origin, others say mystics met to create the cards in the city of Fez which came to prominence sometime after the burning of the great Library of Alexandria. We do know that they first appear in Europe in the latter 14th century as playing cards which is coincidentally about the same time era of Shakespeare's *Henry* plays.

| Foolishness by Giotto, 1306 | The Fool, Visconti-Sforza, 1450 | Joker card, modern deck |

The story enacted in the cards starts with the image of an androgynous youth poised on the edge of a mountain cliff and dressed in the colorful motley of the fool as in folk and court traditions. With a serene expression of equanimity, he gazes upward at a distant height and seems unconcerned that he is about to fall off a cliff. To say the least, he is about to experience something new!

Things are not what they seem. Here on an isolated mountaintop, a place usually reserved for the sage, we find instead a fool on the threshold of possibility, about to incarnate into a new adventure–from the spiritual heights down into the valley of the material world. The card implies that when starting something new, it is wise to be a fool. With a willingness to go forth, he knows nothing but has faith in his own powers of being. Furthermore, the card is assigned the ordinal number zero as a point of origin. The Fool is no negative cipher but possesses all the richness of zero, the freedom of no limitations.

Almost endless are the associations that can be attributed to the image of the Fool. Like any enduring symbol, it has an open-ended quality which accrues new meanings over time. In many spiritual traditions, before the beginning of time, before the Fool can fall into the world, the breath of the spirit must exhale a world into being. So, it seems to me that the Tarot series begins with that foundational metaphor, the breath is the spirit, for the Fool represents that animating energy which gives life. The English word spirit comes from the Latin *spiritus* meaning breath, breath of a god, (inspiration!) from *spirare* to breathe. Numerous other examples exist. The Greek *pneuma* is the vital spirit, soul, or creative force of a person, literally "that which is breathed or blown." In

Hinduism, the Sanskrit word *prana* means the breath of life, the breath of the universe. In Hebrew and Arabic, the *Ruh* is the name for the vital principle of spirit as breath. The *chi* (or *qi* or *ki*) thought of in Chinese medicine as the life force whose movement through the body is the basis of health, has its root in the Mandarin word *qì*, literally "air, breath."

How exactly does the Tarot Fool fit into all of this? Besides being numbered zero, that is, existing before the beginning as only a spirit could do, the concept of zero also connects with breath of wind. Zero derives from the Italian *zefiro* from Medieval Latin *zephirum* or *zephyr,* the light pleasant west wind, almost nothing. And the source of all of this is the Arabic *sifr* or zero, cipher, which was a translation of the Sanskrit *sunya*, meaning emptiness or the void. From this void, all creation arises and returns, the nothing *behind* existence yet which mystics claim is "manifested in every-thing." Thus nothing gets a symbol, not the round "O" but the oval shaped

The World Tarot card, Rider–Waite-Smith deck, 1909

"0." As Theseus says in *Midsummer's Night Dream*, the human imagination gives "to airy nothing / A local habitation and a name."

In the Tarot, the summation of the Fool's adventure is found in the concluding card named the World. Here the life force is imaged as the Cosmic Dancer dancing on the airy nothing of the winds up in the blue vault of the heavens. In the wisdom that the cards have to teach us, She inhabits as if in a cartouche, the middle of a green wreath woven into the shape of zero. Freely dancing on air, She is balanced at the center of zero.

And in the magic of words, further study shows that the origin of the word fool is from the Old French *fol* "fool, foolish," from Latin *follis* "bellows," and by extension, a windbag, an "empty-headed person." A bellows blows air to ignite a fire and has sides that allow it to expand and contract like a human body which takes in a breath to fire our bodies with oxygen and then exhales. Thus the etymology of the word fool connects it to the medieval fool whose "empty headed" jests gives him the freedom to enliven the royal court and to the motif of spirit as the breath of life.

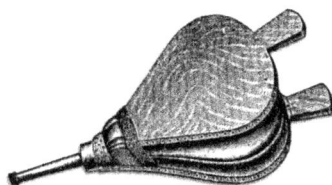

I was there on the day my goddess daughters were born. From my place in the hospital corridor, I waited.

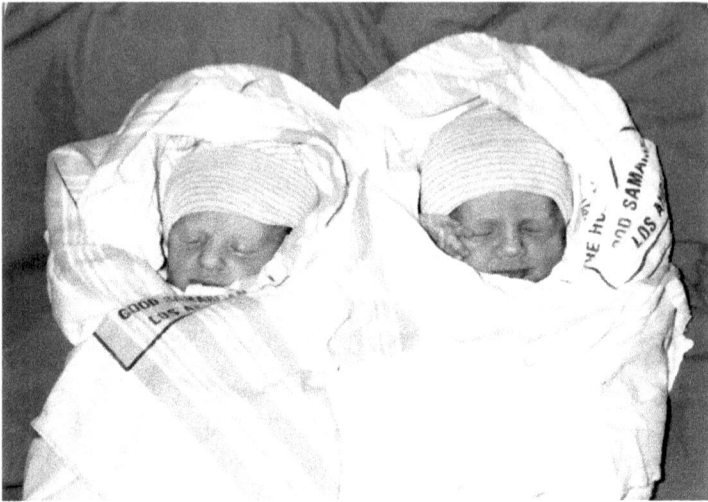

Beyond the wall, inside a room, their mother was giving birth. Suddenly, the sound of a cry astonished me, and then another. Nothing could have announced their presence in this world more to me than those first loud exhalations of breath. To hear it felt like an unbreakable bond between us. They had begun their fool's journey a moment before with their first intake of breath. Much has been said about the rhythm of human breath. Meditation masters teach attention to the movement of our breath is one of the grandest tools we have for coming into the present and for restoring us back to who we really are. Back, they say, to some spark of ourselves before all the layers of socialization strangled us; back, they say, to the freedom to be ourselves.

The Fool shows us the way. Perhaps it's an ideal more often than the real, but his essence we carry inside ourselves as we move through the adventure of being alive. Buoyant, young at heart, creative, the part of us that still feels free and enjoys life. Just like the freedom that Falstaff claims in scene after scene to be himself–the very opposite of the character Babbitt who reveals at the end of the novel, "I never did one thing I wanted to do." Or to the kind of work Thoreau describes which gives a person "no time to be anything but a machine." Far from the stoic endurance of grim duty or the view of life as a dreary series of lessons to be learned, is the lightness of spirit that is the Fool.

By Shakespeare's time in the late 16th century, to be a fool could be a job description. One could be the official fool and be paid for it. What an era! Noble households employed fools for the pleasure of their company. Wit was a commodity. It is said that Henry the VIII's fool, Will Sommers, rarely left the king's side. Artist Hans Holbein included a portrait of him as part of family life. The verbal ingenuity of these learned or "artificial" fools gave them a privileged tongue to tell the truth but tell it at a slant through riddles, song, and rime.

Henry VIII with his jester and his children

Set apart by their special costume made of motley green cloth (it was illegal for an ordinary person to imperson-

A Court Fool, 1552

ate a fool!), these court jesters with their delight in folly had a rare freedom to be themselves and still keep their heads. They stand with one foot outside the social order, but by evoking laughter, fools can make moral commentary on the life they see about them. Through *his* folly, the fool exposes folly *in others*. A second category of fools also existed in wealthy households, the "naturals" or idiot-fools who were mentally handicapped, but revered for their merry antics and moments of innocent wisdom. There was a rare meritocracy in the profession; anyone could be a fool: women, those from the lower classes. All one needed was ability. Thus the Fool moves from archetype to physical embodiment in the domestic fool-for-hire.

Of course, the history of professional fools stretches back thousands of years. There are records of fools in the courts of Egypt as early as 2200 BCE and in places as far ranging as the temple of the of Aztec king Montezuma, to classical Rome where the Emperor Augustus had a fool named Galba. A recent book, *Fools Are Everywhere: The Court Jester Around the World*, demonstrates the seemingly universal need of people for the fool and his humanizing influence on cultures independent of each other around the globe. The book tells the stories of numerous fools: Birbal the Court Jester to the Indian Mogul emperor Akbar and Abu Dulawa the Arab jester poet or the Chinese jester Shi who during the reign of

Archee, the Kinges Iester

Archee Armstrong,
the king's jester, c. 1630-1640

King Huiwang (7th century BCE) gave the perfect fool's cover for verbal license, "I am a jester, my words can give no offense."

Raja Birbal

Buffoon playing a Lute, c. 1623

Miniature *Fête des Fous*, 14th c.

Back to medieval times in England, we find the fool as a rustic clown or buffoon in burlesque folk festivals such as the Feast of Fools celebrated around New Year's Day. Often held in churches and later in the streets, this sanctioned merry-making and drunken partying temporarily disrupted the usual social hierarchy. In a reversal of power, the lower could command the higher. During this ritualized overthrow of order, an elected Lord of Misrule, a kind of Holy Fool, often a peasant, oversaw the Christmas and New Year's festivities. This once a year release of the steam of social resentments had a forbear in the wild revelries of the Roman Saturnalia where slaves and masters switched places. All these festivals mark in one way or another the winter solstice and a return of the growing light, the rebirth of the sun.

The Lord of Misrule

Just as laughter erupts from a reversal of expectations, part of the mystique of the fool exists in surprises, reversals summed up in the phrase, "the wisdom of the fool." Or as poet William Blake advises in the spirited *Proverbs of Hell*, "If the fool would persist in his folly he would become wise." Alas, the custom of the court fool comes to an end by the 18th century. Dicky Pierce, the Earl of Suffolk's fool, died in 1728, the last known household fool in England. An epitaph by Jonathan Swift is engraved on his tombstone.

In the Age of Reason, under the oppressive sway of rationality, there seems to be no room for a fool. But despite shifting customs, the traditions of millennia do not die easily. Nothing as deep in the human psyche as the energies of the Fool can be wiped out completely. Witness our still celebrated April Fool's Day, the movies of Jerry Lewis, Ernest (*Scared Stupid!*), Jack Black, or my favorite TV character as a child, the lovable beatnik Maynard G. Krebs who also stands outside the social order as he speaks his truth with the classic fool's caveat, "No offense, good buddy." Many Americans get the nation's news from late night TV comedian/fools like Dave or Jay or Jon Stewart. And there is that wise learned fool the Great Gorino, Gore Vidal, who wants to wake us citizens up through his ironic commentary, "We have an empire, but none of our students can find it on a map." All these are but to name a few.

"His folly serv'd to make folks laugh"

Maynard G. Krebs

A young Gorino

Still, no one has immortalized the role of the fool more than Shakespeare. There exists no better place than his plays to see the fool in action as companion, trickster, exposer of folly. Most memorable are that great trio of fools, Touchstone in *As You Like It*, Feste in *Twelfth Night* and the Fool in *King Lear*. The addition of gifted comic Robert Armin to the acting troupe may have inspired the Bard to create these roles. (Armin later penned his own book *Foole upon Foole*.) Shakespeare turns away from the old stage tradition of the rustic clown to introduce the court fool as a new character. Thus Armin dons the costume of the professional fool—a coat of motley. In the eccentric book *Shakespeare's Motley*, Englishman Leslie Hobson devotes 300 pages to what the word motley might mean. (Such is the devotion that Shakespeare excites!) Hobson proves how the plays break new ground by shifting from buffoon's russet jerkin to the fool's long coat of motley.

Certainly Shakespeare's explorations of the fool and obvious affinity for this character represent the fool's highest moments, his literary apotheosis. In 1599, the witty fool Touchstone (played by Armin) first appears on the stage in *As You Like It* as a duplicitous trickster, seducer of shepherdesses, and still part clown. After meeting Touchstone in the forest of Arden, the melancholy Jacques envies the fool his freedom: "Invest me in my motley; give me leave / To speak my mind." The splendid Feste, licensed fool to the household of Lady Olivia, finds himself in the center of the whirling atmosphere created by the mad revels of *Twelfth Night*. Also known as the feast of the Epiphany (twelve nights after Christmas), a fool might feel right at home in such an ambiance as this is another New Year's celebration like the Feast of Fools or Saturnalia. Literary critic Harold Bloom observes, "The genius of *Twelfth Night* is Feste, the most charming of all Shakespeare's fools, and the only sane character in a wild play." After a quick paced exchange with Feste, Viola remarks, "This fellow is wise enough to play the

Twelfth Night merry making

fool, / And to do that well craves a kind of wit." Feste, alone on the stage, closes the play with a song reflecting life's uncertainties; the jester also knows the other side: "For the rain it raineth every day."

Feste sings to the melancholy Duke

Finally, we come to the incomparable Fool of Lear, a childlike "natural" fool known for his affections of the heart. He pines away for Cordelia and loves Lear and "labors to outjest his heartstruck injuries" as a gentleman puts it to Kent out on the heath. Or perhaps, as Bloom believes, the Fool torments the king into insanity as punishment for his moral lapses as a father: "Thou shouldst not have been old till thou hadst been wise."

King Lear and the Fool in the Storm

Once Lear has collapsed into this state madness (become his own fool?), the Fool disappears back into the ether or whatever world he came from. I think sometimes the Fool just couldn't take it anymore; he'd had it with Lear's lethal personality.

King Lear and the Fool

If the essence of the fool is his freedom of wit, the two strongest mentalities of any of Shakespeare's characters are Hamlet and Falstaff. From that most intelligent of writers, his most intelligent characters. Both of them play the fool. Hamlet acts the fool when he puts on an "antic disposition," to feign madness as a cover for his designs of revenge and murder. Ah, that second scene of the second act, the conversations with those spies Polonius, Rosencrantz and Guildenstern, what gems of wit and philosophic depth await the reader, what a dazzle of words, of mocking puns, and metaphoric leaps! The young prince takes on the persona of a natural fool with a diseased mind but with the soaring wit of the artificial fool: "I am but mad north-northwest. When the wind is southerly, I know a hawk from a handsaw."

One New Year's Eve with the thought of doing myself some good, I forced myself to sit through a screening of *The Secret*–touting itself as containing, oh, the occult wisdom of the ages known only to a few. What great secret is revealed? Our thoughts make our reality. This is new? Hamlet said some four hundred years ago, "For there is nothing either good or bad but thinking makes it so."

Hamlet ponders all through the play about the brevity of life, the nature of human beings, "this quintessence of dust." Never more so than in that graveyard when he famously holds in his hand the skull of the King's jester:

> Alas, poor Yorick! I knew him, Horatio. A fellow
> of infinite jest, of most excellent fancy. He hath
> bore me on his back a thousand times. And
> now how abhorred in my imagination it is! My

Herbert Beerbohm Tree as Hamlet, 1892 Sarah Bernhardt as Hamlet, c. 1880

gorge rises at it. Here hung those lips that I have kissed I know not how oft. Where be your gibes now? Your gambols, your songs, your flashes of merriment that were wont to set the table on a roar?

Here we see a detailed portrait of the King's fool integrated in the family life of a noble household, the jokes, the kisses, the entertaining conviviality, the warmth. Indeed, is there any other character that Hamlet speaks of with such affection?

"He hath bore me on his back a thousand times"

Many times in both *Henry* plays, Falstaff is called a fool and almost always acts the fool as he is the embodiment of wit. After surviving the civil war due to *his* notion of valor, Sir John vows to "live cleanly as a nobleman should do." But we know this pledge to virtue echoes St. Augustine's prayer, "Oh God make me good...but not yet." For the very next time we see him, much to our delight (for who wants a reformed Falstaff?), he is fully himself. Walking down a London street, having just ordered on credit a satin cloak and breeches for himself, Falstaff muses on his powers of invention: "I am not only witty in myself, but the cause that wit is in other men." He then encounters the Lord Chief Justice, highest law official in the land, who implicates him in the midnight robbery at Gadshill and threatens to put him in the stocks. Far from being cowed, the fat knight hits him up for a thousand pounds. When the Justice accuses him of being an old, burned out case, Falstaff claims to be young, having just been born this very day at three in the afternoon. The spirit of the fool, devoted to play in any circumstance, is ever young, ever being born again.

Falstaff lives. One of his greatest contributions to the play is to stop the juggernaut of war, if just for a moment. In the thick of battle, Prince Henry, hot for revenge, calls upon Falstaff to lend him a weapon; the old man pulls from the holster not a pistol but a bottle of sack. Hal hurls it back at the knight: "What! is't a time to jest and dally now?"

Here Falstaff asserts his formidable personality. What better time to be a jester than in the face of danger? The violence that follows from the prince's concept of honor, the "grinning honor" of the dead have no sway over him. Falstaff wants to live. One can recall another condemning speech about heroics from the most famous warrior who chose to die for glory, Achilles. One can recall in *The Odyssey* the voice of Achilles from Hell:

> I'd rather slave on earth for another man—
> some dirt-poor tenant farmer who scrapes to keep
>   alive—
> than rule down here over all the breathless dead.

One can never hope to understand all the mysteries of the many sided Fool. Nor does this even seem a desirable goal. The archetype of the Fool is an instinctual energy inside us. And yet to me, it hardly seems real that at one time, living breathing men and women were hired to be fools, treasured as a necessary part of culture. Although I know I carry my Fool inside me, sometimes I can't help but wish he were out walking beside me in all his colorful garb.

Courtice Pounds as Feste, 1901

In my life, I have suffered from anxiety and yearned for freedom. I am not alone in experiencing vacillating moods of despair and happiness. But whether my spirit feels heavy or light, I want my Fool there to give perspective on either extreme. Psychiatrist Carl Jung advises that "Not for a moment dare we succumb to the illusion that an archetype can be finally explained and disposed of...The most we can do is to *dream the myth onwards* and give it modern dress."

The Art of Living

Dino

The Art of Living

When did I start loving Dean? I remember as a child watching his weekly TV variety show. He was so much fun and so free–the bungled jokes, the relaxed atmosphere, the songs. It was one of the few things that both my parents and I liked. Half a lifetime later, when my aunt died, I drove down to her house to sort through her belongings. As I entered her home, I felt no residing spirit to make it a cohesive whole; the place was a collection of things fragmented into boxes. From a small container I grabbed up a CD that caught my attention: *Dean Martin, the Collector's Series.* "Oh yes," I smiled. Weeks later, I listened to the music while taking a morning shower. As the luscious water poured over me to the sounds of "That's Amore," "Return to Me," and, at the height of his craft, "Memories Are Made of This," a love flooded over me, a sensation through the nervous system that signaled, here is a great artist. Dino! Then the thought from out of nowhere: he is a modern Falstaff, a Falstaff of our times.

I feel about him how I feel about Falstaff, when is he going to return to the stage to delight me? The very incarnation of the pleasure principle, he seems so happy, he makes us happy. Rat Pack member Joey Bishop said that he did not know of "any performer being as instantly loved when he came on the stage as Dean Martin." Surely part of his appeal is that he likes himself. He radiates an ease of well-being, physical and spiritual. For us in the audience, he lives in a state of grace, free to be himself. The producer of his long-running TV series observed: "Dean knows one thing very well, and better than anyone else. He knows how to be Dean Martin." It made him a star of the brightest magnitude blazing with life force energy as a singer, comedian, actor. But he wore his success lightly with an off-the-cuff casualness and elusiveness, and like any great icon, he remains slightly outside the realm of our understanding.

One person who knew him as well as anyone could is Jerry Lewis, his partner for ten years. That Dino aligned himself with one of the most annoying fools in the history of the arts certainly is a testament to his laid-back cool, and for a while, together they did make magic.

Dean and Jerry, 1955

By 1950, the comedy team of Martin & Lewis had become the highest paid act in show business. In the uptight 50s, America needed the renewing spirit of the Fool! Jerry makes the claim that:

> In the age of Truman, Eisenhower, and Joe McCarthy, we freed America...You have to remember: Postwar America was a very buttoned-up nation. Radio shows were run by censors...We came straight out of the blue- nobody was expecting anything like Martin and Lewis. A sexy guy and a monkey is how some people saw us, but what we really were, in an age of Freudian self-realization, was the explosion of the show-business id.

Martin & Lewis, 1948

In the balance of things, the pleasure principle must assert itself once again especially after one of the most oppressive manifestations of the reality principle, namely World War II. People initially after the war may have longed for a compensating order, but the bottled up id as Lewis put it, must finally burst forth. The passion for life must return. In a review of their 1950 Copacabana show (which broke the club's attendance record), one critic calls them an "amiable pair of clowns," but warns, "Don't ask me to remember what they do, for much of their nonsense doesn't make much sense." Jerry puts it simply, "Audiences went nuts for us."

Audiences responded to the fun that Dean and Jerry generated with their chaos. While other comedians followed a set routine, Martin & Lewis's act was pandemonium; it bristled with a freedom that broke through the bounds of propriety. Jerry recalls that "at any minute absolutely anything could happen. Our wildness, our unpredictability, were a part of the package. It was thrilling to an audience that we could do all the mischievous things they might imagine but would never really do." For Martin, meeting Lewis activated an anarchy deep in his own personality; the lunacy in Jerry was matched by something akin in himself. Dino embraced his fool, and it liberated him.

Before their now-famous first show at the 500 Club in Atlantic City in July 1946, Dean had a mediocre singing career and Jerry's act consisted of putting on a fright wig and lip-syncing to Carmen Miranda records. But together, they had an instant, meteoric success. Lines waited around the block to see their shows and in the months that followed, their salaries skyrocketed from a few hundred bucks a week to $5,000, and by the end of the 1940s to $250,000 a week, to the "top money act" in the business. (What would be the equivalent to such salaries today?) When Martin & Lewis played the Paramount Theater on Broadway, a crowd of 75,000 people filled Times Square hoping to get tickets. I watched an old news reel of Dean and Jerry leaning out a window throwing signed photographs down to the New York City crowd. Their faces had an expression of stunned amazement, not the countenance of hardened show biz veterans, but two young men in a moment of awe at where their fate had taken them.

In an era of conformity, Martin & Lewis shocked and excited their audiences with their jazz-like improvisations and the madness of their slapstick. However, entertaining the audiences came second; primary for the boys was entertaining themselves. An older, subdued Dean remembers those times: "The appeal was we never looked at the audience. We worked to each other."

Jerry too insists on the importance of the bond between the partners: "The love we had for each other is what made that thing work." This trust allowed them to conjure up things out of the air, and audiences shared the "obvious pleasure they felt in performing together." The sexy guy and the monkey, the playboy and the putz, the drill sergeant and the recruit. They worked from a bare-bones script to be tossed aside as the impulse arose. The act flowed from the chemistry of their entwined personalities. Dean comes out on stage and sings smoothly, only to be interrupted by the antics of Jerry's entrance, knocking over busboy's trays and tables. Dean's suave presence balances the loose cannon of Jerry's insatiable need for attention. Both have a joyful mischief in their hearts. Film critic and auteur theorist Andrew Sarris once said the two of them had an "incomparable incompatibility." Comedian Martin Short calls them "The Beatles of Comedy."

Watching old TV clips and movies, one thing strikes me again and again, their physical intimacy.

So free in their spirits, they also seem so free with their bodies. Dean leans into Jerry and rests a hand on his shoulder, a rare moment of repose. Then the frenzy begins again, he sticks his fingers in Jerry's mouth to shut him up. They take turns pouring water over each other's heads and collapse down onto the floor in laughter, their arms thrown carelessly over one another. Dean cocks his fist as if he's going to slug Jerry. Jerry kisses Dean on the lips. Jerry sits on Dean's lap and pretends to be a ventriloquist's dummy. On the 1952 cover of *Look* magazine, their heads tilt to touch with the caption below, "Martin & Lewis, Slapstick with Sex Appeal." Maybe Jerry is right, maybe they did love each other. They certainly were inseparably together for ten years, on the road, backstage, onstage, radio, TV, movies, making millions.

In his book *Dean and Me: A Love Story,* written 50 years after their act broke up and ten years after Dean's death, Jerry needs to get his view of their relationship on the record. His one insistent plea: it's a love story. As an only child abandoned by show biz parents, maybe he felt lovable at last when Dean accepted him. What made them tick is an unanswerable question, but Jerry believes no comedy team could compare with Martin & Lewis.

Hope and Crosby

For example, Crosby and Hope were two skilled performers, but says Jerry, "I don't think that deep down the two men particularly like each other, and I believe that deep down, it showed...Crosby and Hope never generated anything like the hysteria that Dean and I did and that was because we had that X factor, the powerful feeling between us...a kind of mystery." On stage or in the movies, Jerry seems perpetually smitten with Dean, with the mere pleasure of his physical presence.

Jerry was only 19 and Dean a decade older at 29 when they met. Over the years, Jerry's worship remains the same: "I adored Dean. He was a big brother to me. He was charming, bigger than life. I was in awe of him." They were first introduced to each other at the corner of Broadway and 54th in March 1946. Jerry remembers the mesmerizing impact of Dean's charisma, "I thought, 'How does anybody get that handsome?' I couldn't take my eyes off him."

Supremely needy, Jerry badly wants a friend; he looks to Dean, the meta master of cool who knows more of the world and can protect him. In one form or another, in their stage act and in their inferior movies (which could never capture the dynamism of their live performances), this relationship plays out.

At War with the Army, one of the biggest grossing films of 1950

Hosting *The Colgate Comedy Hour*, they part the stage curtain and walk forward, arm in arm. Dean sings, "Partners, we belong together," and Jerry adds, "We do

Hosts of *The Colgate Comedy Hour*, 1950-1955
Rosemary Clooney and the boys

things together." Free to have the most fun two guys could have; that's their legacy, according to Lewis.

Yet, every light casts a shadow, and ten years to the day, in July 1956, the end came for Martin & Lewis when they performed together for the last time at the Copacabana. Two years earlier on a TV show, in a revealing skit, Dean is having a nervous breakdown; everybody is becoming Jerry Lewis! People walking down the street, cops, cab drivers. At home, Jerry is in every room of his house. He tells a friend, "This little monster I'm workin' with is driving me crazy. We're workin' in nightclubs, I see him seven nights a week; we make pictures, I see him everyday... he's got me crazy, I don't know what to do." He then confides

his troubles to a shrink who also turns into Jerry. As there is no escape, Dean tries to kill Jerry. Later, Lewis says they'd never have broken up if it weren't for meddling outside influences, but clearly Dean had had it. Jerry's frenetic mania became too much even for him; can't a fellow finish a song? As Bosley Crowther in a 1953 *New York Times* movie review of *The Caddy* observes, "Mr. Lewis is slowly taking over." But as Dean withdrew, Jerry's desperate needs escalated. One astounding performance is a neat compendium of their tensions. Dean on stage, sings his great hit "That's Amore" (from *The Caddy* and nominated for an Academy Award). Jerry has the cameraman close in on Dean, distorting his features. Then Jerry climbs up behind Dean, starts pulling his hair while crying, "You're all mine, you're mine." Dean winces from the pain, his face contorts in anger, "Jer, you're overacting. It's over. It's over."

Even though Jerry lauds Dean after their split as the backbone of the act, and as "one of the great comic talents of our time," Martin believed that he didn't get the credit he deserved. He felt "like a stooge" and increasingly embarrassed by Jerry.

A glimpse of what Dean had to put up with

Besides these sensitive subjects, he wanted to see how far he could go on his own, to find out what he was capable of. "Dean just felt he would have been better on his own," says wife Jeanne Martin. Following his maxim that "your life is your own," he became a solo act. Decades later, Dean recounts a tense, final meeting at Paramount, which was kept afloat by the surreal Martin & Lewis films. The studio heads threatened him, "You can't walk out on thirty million dollars." To which Dean replied, "Well, you just watch me." He believed that ahead for him, "there'll be more." And, he thought he was funnier than Jerry.

He was not alone in that perception of being the greater wit. Bud Yorkin, director from their hit TV show, *The Colgate Comedy Hour*, believes that "Relaxed with no temperament, Dean was the funnier of the two, came up with the funnier lines. The crew loved Dean." Shirley MacLaine, who worked with the boys in one of their best movies, *Artists and Models*, and later as part of the Rat Pack, says, "To my surprise, Dean, not Jerry, was the funny one to me. His humor was subtle, spontaneous–a result of the moment. Jerry's was brilliant, but usually premeditated." Angie Dickinson, who starred with Dean in one of his greatest roles in *Rio Bravo*, concurs: "Dean is a very, very funny man, naturally amusing, like Charlie Chaplin. He did normal things, and they were hysterical. Whereas Jerry tried to be funny, Dean just is *funny*."

Equipped with gifts and the means to realize them, the dawn of the Golden Age of Dino began! When he threw off the bondage of that external fool, Jerry, Dino was free to become his own lovable Fool, whose ease of being gave new meaning to the word *relaxed*. In the years to come, he made critically acclaimed movies with the greatest actors of the time, had a phenomenal solo nightclub career and as a member of the Rat Pack, recorded numerous hit records, and for almost a decade had one of the top shows on TV. Dino became the most popular entertainer in the world.

Dean's star for film on Hollywood Stars Walk of Fame, he had additional stars for music and for television

Even today, one would be hard pressed to think of a performer as successful in as many fields of entertainment. In a class by himself, he is universally loved, but he doesn't seem to care.

The character of Dino may be as much an artifice as the character of Falstaff, but to me, both seem like real personalities I relish spending time with on the page or in the theater, or through movies and music, or just by thinking about them. When Martin needed a new way to present himself to the public, he exaggerated certain innate qualities to become Dino: his always-up-for-play nature and love of song, spirits, and women. In 1957, his solo act first premiered at the Sands in Las Vegas. What courage it must have taken to walk out alone into those harsh stage lights and face the waiting audience of Hollywood elites. (Later he called it one of the biggest moments of his life.)

March 6, 1957, Copa Room in Las Vegas

Yet Dino exists in another world of his own making, outside the bounds of everyday consequences, free from the savage attacks of the superego; he lives for pleasure. With his consciousness perpetually altered by drink, he seems to be lifted an inch off the stage, not subject to the laws of gravity or oppressive cares like the rest of us poor stiffs. Thankfully, he invites us in to join the fun. Away with the machine of duty, come back to us, O Spirit of Delight!

But there was more inside him than just this; we cannot sum up Dino with a fixed identity. Instead, the enigma of surprising depths surfaces. Even Jeanne, his wife of 24 years, confesses, "The important thing to say about my husband is this: I don't understand him. Nobody does. There is something inside him that is unreachable." Such as the unexpected desire that arose from somewhere inside him, that after 16 silly movies with Jerry, "I wanted to be in serious pictures. I knew I could do it, I knew." After initial missteps, he began, in 1958, a trio of movies: *The Young Lions*, *Some Came Running*, and my personal favorite, *Rio Bravo*. These cemented his reputation as a dramatic actor. His old nemesis at *The New York Times*, Bosley Crowther, wrote that no one was more surprised than he at Martin's skills. On the set of *The Young Lions*, Dino's sunny nature eased the titanic battle of egos between Montgomery Clift and Marlon Brando.

To both, Dean seemed a natural. Whatever fears he may have had, he seized this opportunity, telling his agent he'd "play the role for free" (which, at a salary of $20,000, was practically free for him, as it was less than a week's work at the Sands). The film's director, Edward Dmytryk, knew that "he could rise to the occasion...I mean after Jerry Lewis, why would he be afraid to stand up to Brando or Clift?"

Touted as an antiwar film, Dino, as Broadway star and draft dodger Michael Whiteacre delivers the picture's best line: "Look, I've read all the books. I know that in 10 years we'll be bosom friends with the Germans and the Japanese. Then I'll be pretty annoyed that I was killed." I like that the film doesn't feel the need to later transform

Frank Sinatra and Dean (as Bama), two characters meet in a bar

him into a sacrificial hero as punishment for his devotion to life or for showing the common sense of Falstaff on the battlefield.

In his next role as the drunken gambler Bama in *Some Came Running*, he played off his languid style with humor and an ironic distance from the events of the plot. Both films made the top ten lists of 1958 as critical and box-office successes. Dino, in two of the biggest movies of the year, was on his way, making a huge comeback to an unprecedented second career.

But to my mind, the best was yet to come: his performance as Dude in *Rio Bravo*. The plot, who cares? Something about an evil rancher trying to take over the town, opposed by Sheriff John Wayne and his drunken deputy Dude/Dino. Then there's also Walter Brennan and Ricky Nelson on the team, a strange cast for a western, what? My sole concern: will Dino make it to the end of the movie alive? Must his crooked road to recovery and heroism also include his death? This seems to me the central tension of the plot—not what might happen to that stinkin' town. By the end, Dino once again escapes the wrath of the superego and puritan goodness—maybe that's why we love him so much—maybe there's relief for us too.

But how he suffers in the course of the film and how we suffer along with him. In his anguish at drying out in order to become the sharp-shooter he once was, Dino's

skillful performance dares all, revealing the shadow side of his happy-go-lucky drunk persona. The movie starts with an image of Dude apprehensive, rubbing his face as he enters a saloon. Dirty, disheveled, so desperate for a drink, he would willingly put his hand in a spittoon to retrieve the silver dollar that will buy him another shot. When we see him next, he wears a badge; Sheriff John Wayne has plucked him from the depths of humiliation for a chance to regain his lost self. Not invincible like the Duke, Dude pounds on his own knee just to feel something other than the pain of addiction. All his human failures and wrong decisions manifest in the film's only close-up: Dino shaking as he tries to roll a cigarette, "What can a man do with hands like that?" These trials cleanse and strengthen him for his redemption in the movie's big showdown. When the last image fades to black, Dude walks tall down Main Street as the voice of Dino sings over the credits, "While the *Rio Bravo* rolls along...." If any other character was present, I don't remember. He is the very heart of the film and the reason why we care.

The next year, 1960, saw the release of *Who Was That Lady?*, one of his most delicious comic roles that his fans relish as it lifts the spirit when Dino evades the drab duty of doing the right thing. Unlike some of his later comedies, it doesn't imprison him in the end with "sincere" feelings and

A light-hearted leer at love among the adults!

TONY CURTIS · DEAN MARTIN · JANET LEIGH

Who was that Lady?

JAMES WHITMORE · JOHN McINTIRE · BARBARA NICHOLS

NORMAN KRASNA · GEORGE SIDNEY

matrimony. His lighthearted freedom, which he was so adept at portraying, earned him a Golden Globe nomination. Jeanne remonstrates that we're "fools" if we think it's as easy as he makes it seem. Dino and co-star Tony Curtis work together with deft comic timing when Curtis calls on, of all people, Dino, to help him save his marriage. Janet Leigh plays the beautiful idiot wife who doesn't like Dino: "You're flighty and irresponsible and libertine." He couldn't be more pleased. Dino's raffish personality riffs on marriage: "I can't breathe, all that 'I love you the most.'" I hold in my mind's eye the image of him forever smiling as he drives up in a white convertible, showing off his dark good looks.

By the end of the 1950s, he had become one of the biggest stars on the scene. His records were back on the charts; he was among the most popular performers in Las Vegas; *Rio Bravo* triumphed as one of the top-grossing films of that year. In honor of John Wayne's centenary and its release as a two-set DVD, *Rio Bravo* was presented at the 2007 Cannes Film festival. *Who Was That Lady?* was also

Grauman's Chinese Theater, 1964

brought out recently as a DVD with 1968's *How To Save Your Marriage (And Ruin Your Life)* as "a double shot" of Dean Martin. His next movies were *Bells Are Ringing* with the brilliant Judy Holliday in her last screen role

and then came *Ocean's 11*, the first Rat Pack movie. In it, Dino seems content to stand aside and let Frank Sinatra take the lion's share of the limelight. But he's not diminished by it, not a

whiff of desperation about him unlike Sammy Davis Jr. or Peter Lawford.

The only bearable moments of the film are his make out scene with Shirley MacLaine in a fur coat on the hood of a car. And while the caper's afoot, Dino performs in the lounge, "Ain't That a Kick in the Head...She's picked out a king size bed." Such joy on his face as he croons, "My life is gonna be beautiful."

Dean's sojourn in the Rat Pack cemented his persona of Dino, the swinging King of Cool. The good life full of every kind of pleasure. One critic points out that the rise of anarchic self-indulgence didn't begin in the late 60s with the hippies but was right at the heart of the ethos celebrated by the Rat Pack earlier in the decade.

Rat Pack Confidential author Shawn Levy describes their free-floating world: "There you had them—a group consisting of the nation's greatest and most popular entertainers, with the blessing of a dynamic political star [Jack Kennedy] and fearsome crime lords, the favors of gorgeous women, an enviable playground, all the money in the world." Dino and his pallies (as he called most everybody) continue to attract our attention. Think of the recent movies about the Rat Pack or *Oceans 11, 12, 13.*

Of course, Dino never cared much about what people thought of him—his fans, his friends, the mob.

Frank was in awe of Dean, the only one he couldn't control, the only one who could leave a party early with impunity.

Friends across the decades

Or, like the ancient fool, could speak the truth. Once Frank asked Sammy's girl to strip to her bra and panties to surprise Dean, who soon walks in and says, "Frank's an asshole, put your clothes back on." Dino had powers that eluded Frank. Jeanne recounts Frank wondering to Dean: "How come you always get the laughs and I don't?" Dean tells him: "That's because you're not funny." Or as Dino observes, "Frank takes things seriously; I don't." Witness the Rat Pack's advice to Shirley Maclaine when she was about to start her nightclub career:

>Frank: "Remember one thing baby. You change the room by showing up."
>
>Sammy: "Pull out all the stops."
>
>Dean: "What do you need it for?"

Surely one of the strangest portraits of the persona of Dino can be seen in Billy Wilder's *Kiss Me, Stupid*. In the movie, Dino plays a parody of himself in a weird blurring of the boundaries between life and art; Dino is a singer named Dino who plays Vegas, makes movies, and is a renowned womanizer. Without an ounce of vanity, Dino shows great courage in satirizing himself and according to Wilder, "wasn't the slightest bit embarrassed" to play this caricature. In the story, Dino must escape from Vegas; after his show, numerous chorines set up rendezvous with him, and he says yes to every girl until a stagehand warns, "The German twins are waiting for you in the sauna."

On the road back to Hollywood for his next picture with Frank, he winds up in Climax ("the only way to go"), Nevada. Slightly repellant as a sleaze who only wants to sleep with his host's wife, Dino has to have it every night or else, "I wake up with such a headache." On the set, Dino refused to be intimated by Wilder, then at the height of his career and known to literally drive actors to suicide attempts with his martinet control and hectoring directions. After a complicated set of instructions on how to play the scene, Dino exploded in mock anger, "Well for chrissake, Jesus Christ almighty what the fuck! I mean, if you wanted an actor what the fuck did you get me for? Why didn't

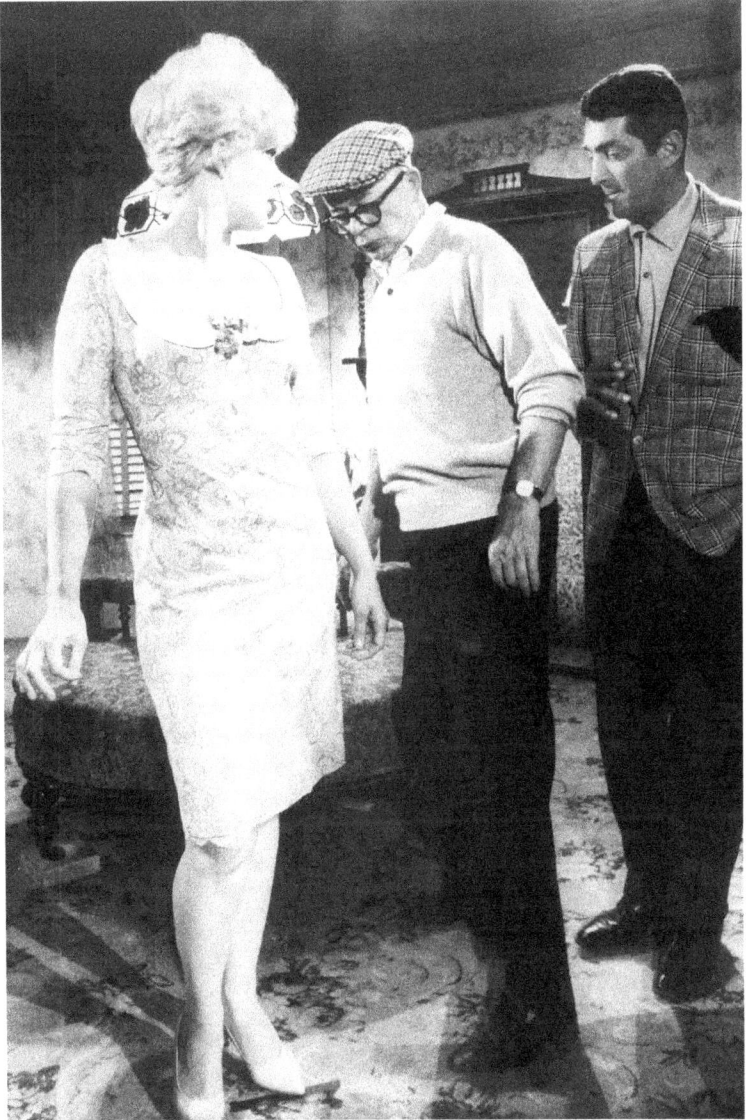

Kim Novak, Billy Wilder, and Dino on set, 1964

you go get fucking Marlon Brando?" Billy loved it. By the end of this bedroom farce and *only* after infidelities have saved the institution of marriage, everyone gets what they want. Songwriter Orville J. Spooner ("Without you, I'm a poached egg without a piece of toast") gets Dino to sing his song on national television. Only Dino has no need of change; his persona remains self-contained.

Kim and Dino relax on location at Twenty-Nine Palms, California

Loathed by the critics, condemned by the Catholic Legion of Decency, the picture bombed. Godly citizens were outraged by the film's vulgarity. Wilder retreated to Europe to escape the uproar while Dino floated forward into his next big adventure, the top-rated show on television that would make him ever more popular and one of the richest men in Hollywood.

The stage at Studio 4 in Burbank is full of guest stars and regular cast members rehearsing, supported by the camera and sound crew, stage managers, musicians, choreographers, directors, but the center is not there. Per his contract, Dino will not appear till Sunday afternoon at the last possible moment, and when he does, he cheerfully inquires, "Is this where the action is?" The crew loves him— they have never been introduced to him, but nevertheless, they love him. Dean must be allowed to breeze in and out without any interruptions. Into his dressing room he goes, watching football games on TV, occasionally glancing at the other monitor, which displays the final blocking of the show. His dressing room is off-limits, even for guests.

He knows nothing: who his guests will be, let alone his lines. Everything in *The Dean Martin Show* centers around its star, keeping it new for him; what is important is that Dean "still enjoy himself, still *be* himself." Finally, it's time;

he appears onstage; the show can begin. He doesn't exhibit the slightest concern that 50 million people watch his show. If he misses a cue, fumbles a lyric, so what? He has no image of self-worth to maintain. Nothing can spoil his fun or disturb his equanimity. He's Dino, a comic fool gliding through his own inebriated world, slightly out of synch with so-called reality. This excuses any and every mishap, and it only makes the audience love him more and wish *they* could be that free.

The show runs on one principle: Dean must not be bored. One could look at not wanting to be bored as superficial, an indictment of someone who can't fix their attention, or, at the loftiest level, one could say Dino wants to be present, alive to all the possibilities of now, of opportunities almost tingling on his skin. Who wants to know ahead of time, to decide about the future? Analyzing, picking it apart over and over—this is deadly boredom. Let's keep it real in the moment, "Hey, pallie, that's beautiful."

The TV show captures the magic of Dino trusting his own instincts. An anything-could-happen atmosphere that recalls his early years with Jerry in their live nightclub act, an act in service to the spontaneous eruptions of the id. That's what keeps his boredom at bay—the thrill of the edge, the adrenaline of not knowing. Because of Dean's ad-libbing, "show timings went out the window. But Dean never bothered with little details like that." A Buddhist master of detachment and serenity, his freedom of expression and his charismatic affinity with his audience and the other performers created his likability, that fun-to-be-around vibe.

Guests on the show
Dino and Sergio Franchi; Arte Johnson, Dino, and Diana Shatz;
Jimmy Stewart, Dino, and Orson Welles

How eager the stars are to appear with him, yet it took nerve. Practically a live show, the cameras never stopped for retakes on Dino's set. It was a tightrope act, and the stakes were high. This week's guest might be a favorite like Orson Welles. Two kindred spirits, he holds Dean in awe as a man who could appear completely unprepared in front of tens of millions of people and still perform with such ease and grace. Welles would say, "The rest of us need to practice, rehearse, not Dean... The guy's got it." Welles, an actor of great technique and soul, played Falstaff in the favorite of all his films, *Chimes at Midnight*. (Falstaff and Dino meet!) In one memorable appearance on the show, Welles explains the character of Falstaff to the audience all the while transforming himself with make-up into the fat knight. Then, straight into the camera, he delivers Falstaff's famous soliloquy on the healing properties of drink, of sherry-sack. Welles was also fascinated by Dean who "knows exactly what he's doing and he's getting away with it!"

If Dean is the last to arrive, he is the first to leave. Four hours later, still in his tuxedo, he'd already be driving his Facel Vega home before the closing theme music.

He enjoyed doing TV, but wanted to be free to play golf, and maybe do some movies, record some LPs, perform in clubs. To do what he liked, "Now that's livin', pallie."

He made a fortune from the reruns and even now, lengthy commercials air to sell DVDs of the TV show. Two days before what would have been his 90th birthday, Critic's Choice in *The New York Times* announced the release of new DVDs of yet another set of his movies: "More than half a century has not proved sufficient to solve the mystery of Dean Martin and Jerry Lewis, nor to diminish their appeal."

Recently, at a local library, I'm checking out *Backstage at the Dean Martin Show*. Up to the head of the line, the dull librarian motions me forward. Looking down at the book, she suddenly wakes up, "Oh, I used to watch him, that show when I was ten. I loved staying up late to watch it. It was the bane of my mother's existence. She couldn't make me go to bed." Thursday nights 10 pm, Dean owned the airwaves. I egg her on, "He made you feel good, didn't he?" She replies, "I used to think, 'He's so beautiful.'" I exit with the book, leaving her to float in a radiant memory.

The Dean Martin Show is the capstone of his creative life, nine years of popular and commercial success, which then morphed into the celebrity roasts. The most watched man on TV; certainly the highest paid, especially if you consider he only worked three to four hours a week. And then his decline: his divorce from Jeanne, the years of smoking catching up, the fall into old age, the desire for solitude after losing the love of performing, and most bitter of all, the death of his son, Dino Jr.

It began for him as a singer, his soul essence, a singing Italian. He sums up himself: "What else is there to say about me? I love to sing and I love women." Why *do* humans sing? We hear scientists claim animals do everything from biological necessity, that birds don't sing for the sheer joy of it. We are stingy in our anthropomorphic assignment of pleasure. But isn't play a biological necessity? Everything could be communicated through the normal, ordinary speaking voice, but we don't do that, do we? We have to sing from time to time. It must be an inner urge to express ourselves in a pleasurable way. What does it matter except that we want to do it, and for as far back as we can tell, humans have always been doing it. To sing, you only need your own body, a fool's breath to come in and go out, carrying a vibration of sound. Just that and some desire.

Through his Dino-essence, he views his career: "Look, I sing a song. If it's a hit, beautiful. If it isn't, we try again. Why make it complicated?" In 1964, when he recorded his smash hit "*Everybody Loves Somebody Sometime*," he knocked the Beatles' "A Hard Day's Night" out of the #1 spot on the charts. He then sent the following telegram: "Dear Elvis, If you can't handle the Beatles, I'll do it for us. Dean Martin." The King of Rock n' Roll was a big fan, called Dean his favorite singer. Elvis admired, even idolized Dean's "easy-going, ultra smooth delivery and a hint of the mischievous" as described in *How Elvis was influenced by Dean Martin*. Elvis adopted "Dino's nonchalant way of twisting syllables and slurring notes and became very much part of the Elvis style." In the course of Dino's singing life, he recorded more than 100 albums. In the early 1960s, he had an extraordinary string of 27 top-charted singles, as well as earning

a groundbreaking seven gold albums in an 18-month period. His first number one hit remains my favorite, "Memories Are Made of This." The great documentary, *Dean Martin: The One, The Only* ends with an image of Dino in a live performance singing "Memories Are Made of This" onstage with the Easy Riders providing back-up vocals, guitar, and that descending bass run. Oh, the look on his face, an artist in rapture, the delight of creating such beauty right in that very moment. The son of immigrants from southern Italy who found their way to Steubenville, Ohio, the son who knew, "I just had it in me."

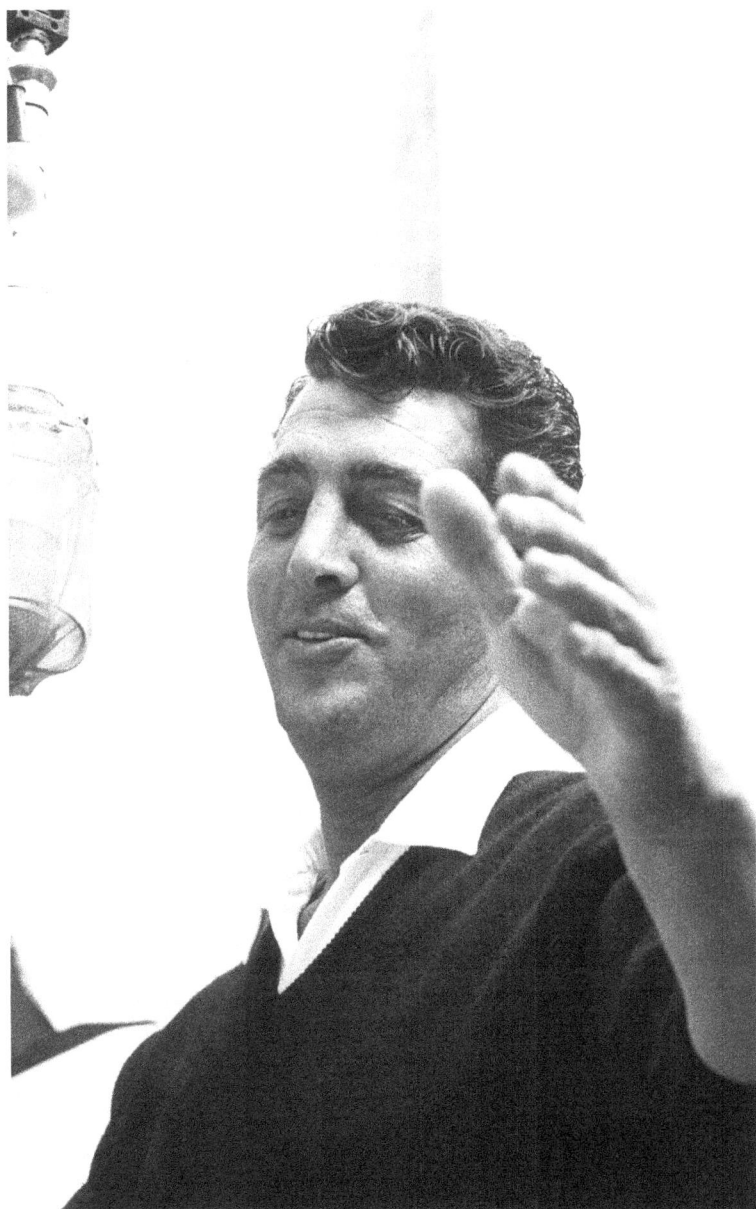

The Art of Living

Epilogue

Falstaff

The Fool

Dino

I cannot live without being in love. I consider that trio of beings, Falstaff, the Fool, and Dino, friends who help me to live. No one is more surprised than I that they have come into my consciousness, that a feminist like myself spends time cultivating a relationship with these males (the Fool is neutral, androgynous). But after the relief from the death of my father, their spirits are what I desired and what I needed. The poet Shelley in his "Invocation" cries out:

> RARELY, rarely, comest thou,
> Spirit of Delight
> Wherefore hast thou left me now
> Many a day and night?
> Many a weary night and day
> 'Tis since thou art fled away.

If, like the poet, one has felt this dry absence, then one can appreciate the necessary balm embodied in these three characters—their delight at being alive. How many of us have longed for their juicy offerings, the blessing of life? In the Sumerian *Epic of Gilgamesh*, the hero rejects his life to endure a fruitless quest to escape death, only to be told by Siduri, priestess of the waters:

> ...fill your belly with good things;
> day and night, night and day,
> dance and be merry,
> feast and rejoice.
> Let your clothes be fresh,
> bathe yourself in water,
> cherish the little child that holds your hand,
> and make your wife happy in your embrace;
> for this too is the lot of man [sic].

Oh, to be like Chaucer's the Wife of Bath when she claims, "That I have had my world as in my tyme." Harold Bloom points out that the Wife of Bath is a literary ancestress to Falstaff just as I have come to see Sir John as a spiritual ancestor to Dino, a man alive in my time.

I've learned through them that it takes courage to rely on your own self, on your own instincts and delights. I started with a single word to sum up the essence of each of these beings: wit, freedom, ease; Falstaff, the Fool, Dino. And I perceive the archetype of the Fool as the foundational energy which sustains the personalities of the other two. Falstaff derives his wit from his freedom to express himself. He answers to no values other than his own, even if the whole social structure stands against him. Likewise, Dino's ease of being, his meta-relaxedness originates from a similar freedom to be himself. He simply doesn't care what others think. Jeanne says no one, nothing, impressed him deeply. He would come home from work; she in her wifeness would ask what happened today? "Oh, nothing," he'd reply. Later she'd turn on the TV news, "The King and Queen of England visited Dean Martin today on his movie set."

We revere them because of this sense of freedom. They believe their lives belong to them. The blessing of life means to be free from a severity of conscience that kills the joy of things. Not for these liberated souls, the tyrannical authority of imposed rules of social conduct. Not for them, the paralyzing, suicidal guilt of the superego. They draw on the vitalizing spirit of play. Falstaff and Dino are performers, amusing themselves as well as others, Fools keeping the Royal Household entertained! By his superior intelligence and dazzling wit, Falstaff transforms the events of his life to public stories around the tavern fires and feasting tables. Dino, a man with innate intelligence and natural wit, as a singer, actor, comedian plays before the biggest audiences in the world. They love the pleasures of life: food, drink, women; capons, pasta fagioli; sherry sack, J&B scotch; Doll Tearsheet, Dino's many romances.

Stańczyk, an introspective court jester

Yet for all of that, they strike me as figures of solitude. The enigma of their personalities is a source of wonder. More has probably been written about Falstaff than any of Shakespeare's characters except for Hamlet. Dino too has outlived his own time through our continued fascination about his life and work. Even so, we can't "pluck out the heart" of their mysteries as Hamlet would say. Both are cool observers of human nature; they perceive truths which set them apart from the rest of us. Only Falstaff resists the empty rhetorics on the glory of war, and Dino knows that John F. Kennedy will abandon the Rat Pack the instant they are no longer of use to him. They manifest the strength of integrity; neither the Prince nor Frank Sinatra can make them go against themselves. For Falstaff and Dino approve of themselves, not in some puffed-up-ego, cock of the walk way, but with a self-acceptance, they enjoy their own stories and songs, take relish in their creative powers. Self-contained, they remain uniquely themselves and finally, unknowable.

Not to say that others don't love them. The bawd Doll Tearsheet loves old Falstaff "better than I love e'er a scurvy young boy of them all." Mistress Quickly remains loyal to the end. I have studied Dino, from sleazy exposés to reputable documentaries,

Falstaff and Doll Tearsheet played by Orson Welles and Jeanne Moreau

and never once, not once, has any stage hand, crew member, actor, actress, director said anything less than they loved working with him, that he was a pleasure to be around, not one, never any less than that.

Mahalia Jackson and Dean, an unlikely pair of singers rehearsing. Did everybody like Dino?

Jerry, Jeanne, his children, who all have cause for complaint, seem remarkably free from bitterness. One hears expressions of love for him, about his sweetness, his easy ways, their gratitude at the lucky fate of having had him in their lives. It's hard to find anyone who really thinks ill of him. In the end, Jeanne affirms, "He left us smiling."

One last sad way that the two align with each other: both Falstaff and Dino die as old men with broken hearts. Both are undone by love. Both experience a supreme goodbye in their old age, the death of an adored son. One metaphoric, one literal. The pain of these losses was sharp, sharp enough to inaugurate one final cycle of life— the decline to death. Not all of Falstaff's wit can save him from misreading the prince, clouded as he is by yearning. What is lost when Prince Hal becomes King Henry V and banishes his old friend from his life? Falstaff loses his Beloved, his dreams of wealth and position; the country loses a part of its past, and the king, in rejecting Falstaff, kills the spirit of delight.

For Falstaff's long scenes at the tavern depict the merry making of drink, talk, tall tales with the lads, music,

Boar's Head Tavern

amorous interludes before the hearth fires of the Boar's Head Tavern.

And in the country scenes at Gloucestershire, set in an orchard under an arbor, a bucolic feast awaits Falstaff and his companions which reveals a life far from internecine power struggles of the court.

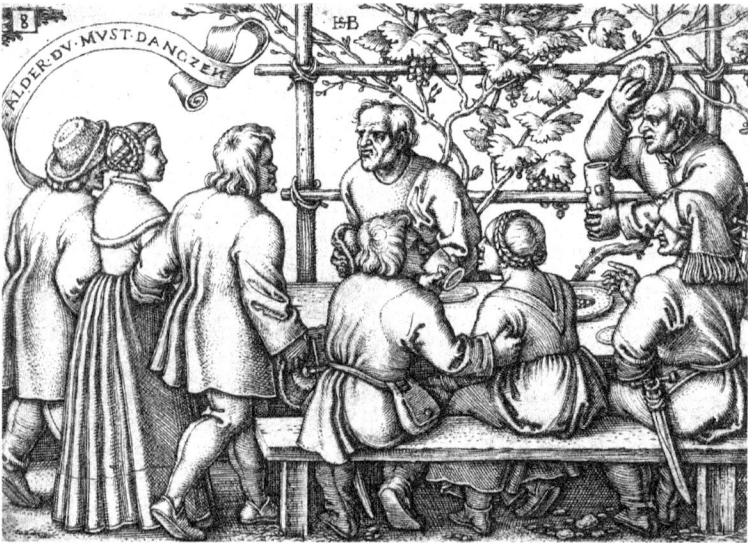

Here is a brief pause between the "civil butchery" brought by Henry IV and the war abroad soon to be launched by his son Henry V. What sane person wouldn't rather be in Master Shallow's garden with a welcome to all, with an abundance of food and wine and song than in the deadly company of the king? Let us "praise God for a merry year" as Falstaff raises a full cup to toast, "Health and long life to you" in another gesture to the blessing of life.

Justice Swallow persuades Falstaff to stay for the night:
"By cock and pie, sir, you shall not away tonight"

When the news comes that the old king has died,
Falstaff, still believing in his intimacy with Prince Hal, exalts
that "the laws of England are at my commandment."

Pistol informs Falstaff of the death of Henry IV

He must leave at once; he knows "the young king is sick for me." After lavish promises to his friends, he charges out for an all night ride to London. There he mixes into the crowd thronged to witness the coronation procession of the new king. From the street, Falstaff cries out: "King Hal; my royal Hal!...God save thee, my sweet boy!... I speak to thee, my heart!" But a cold blooded reply pierces that heart. At last Hal publicly reveals his true nature which we have known from his first soliloquy:

> I know thee not, old man:
> fall to thy prayers. How ill white hairs become a
>   fool and jester!
> I have long dream'd of such a kind of man,...
> But, being awaked, I do despise my dream....
> Reply not to me with a fool-born jest,
> Presume not that I am as I have been,…
> I banish thee, on pain of death,...
> Not to come near our person by ten mile.

Thus he rejects then silences his Fool forever. Many hold the view that by this brutal severance, the young king comes into his sober maturity. The play concludes with the king's ambitious intention to invade France. What are we left with? Gone are the warm fires and rustic green of Merry Old England; the new world order rejects the inconstant moon of Falstaff's magical nights, and in the cold light of day, awakened from the night's dreams, a murderous rationality concerns itself with starting the next war. What we are left with is not the new king's glory but our hearts

The new king abandons his fool

broken with the broken hearted Falstaff. What kind of king banishes from his court the truth telling wit of the Fool?

Although Shakespeare tries to soften the blow in the epilogue by promising the audience to bring Falstaff back to "continue the story," he doesn't do this. How can the comic vision of Falstaff fit into the monstrous efficiency of the new regime? Renaissance scholar Herschel Baker remarks: "Despite his promise...to keep Falstaff alive and let him go to France, Shakespeare really had to kill him off, for Falstaff with his tonic disrespect and his genius for subversion, would have been a greater threat to Henry V than all the French at Agincourt."

Two statues at the Shakespeare Memorial at Stratford-upon-Avon:
Prince Hal takes hold of his crown to ascend to power,
Falstaff contemplates life's delights

All that is left for Falstaff is to die. Such is the power of his personality that we cannot witness this passing firsthand. It must occur offstage; he cannot be allowed in the play. With tender emotion, the faithful Mistress Quickly describes for friends gathered before the Boar's Head Tavern (and for us), how he "went away" as the cold in his feet moved "upward and upward" extinguishing his splendid fire.

His dying process mirrors accounts of how upward, from root to crown, the life force leaves the bodies of yoga masters. Not for Falstaff a eulogy from kings but rather from the dimwitted, warmhearted Mistress, whose garbled misunderstandings of his final words allow us one last laugh with Falstaff even as our tears fall. Mysteriously, he had spoken of "a table of green fields" which Harold Bloom believes is Mistress Quickly's distortion of Falstaff's singing of the Psalm 23: "Thou preparest a table before me" and "to lie down in green pastures." Certainly the fabled green countryside of England also comes to mind (later depicted in Blake's "England's green and pleasant Land"). Sadly, as the good hostess perceives, the great knight perishes because the "The King has kill'd his heart." Falstaff dies not for honor but for love.

Dino, that master performer, also dies offstage in seclusion away from the public eye. This withdrawal from the world began (like for any human being), with the natural processes of the body wearing down. Of course, he wasn't exactly like the rest of us; how many of us are world class artists? Yet, he was always, in a way, indifferent to the external world. Deana Martin in her memoir describes her father as "Happy with his own company and entirely self-contained,...he'd prefer to be silent." Jeanne concurs, "Dean doesn't have an overwhelming desire to be loved. He doesn't give a damn." One critic calls him a "Zen master without a spiritual anchor." Although, his wife testifies that he said his prayers every night, grateful for his many blessings. Later he felt that he had done everything, experienced all of what life had to offer: "I've done it all. I've lived a full life...I have no regrets."

One by one the pleasures of the world evaporated for Dino. I asked a friend who worked at Hillcrest Country Club in Los Angeles for any Dean Martin stories. Once a legendary gambler on the golf course, an older Dean had come out to play. "Mr. Martin, you going to beat these guys today?" Then came the tired reply, "Oh, I don't care anymore." Later he sped out of the club parking lot in his Stutz Blackhawk and almost ran my friend down in the street. His license plate read, "Drunky."

"I wouldn't change one thing, not one thing," Dino claimed in an interview as an older man, but that was before fate delivered a devastating blow. In the spring of 1987, his son Dino Jr., or Dean Paul, a captain in the Air National Guard, while flying a training mission during a freak blizzard, crashed his jet into the side of Mt. San Gorgonio.

Dean Paul, tennis champion

A few years earlier, a plane carrying Frank Sinatra's mother (on her way to see Frank in Las Vegas) had fatally crashed into this same mountain. Dean Paul, incredibly handsome, an actor, a gifted athlete, captain in the guard, when asked once about being Dean Martin's son, said: "There is no way that my father is going to sit down and open up...I don't know him very well at all." But in his own remote way, I think Dino was proud of him. The family had an agonizing wait of four days before the body was found. They even consulted a psychic supplied by old friend Shirley MacLaine to help find the remains. President Reagan ordered an SR-71 spy plane to photograph the search area.

At the funeral, Deana, who sat behind her father, writes, "That was the only time I ever saw my father cry. His shoulders shook violently as he collapsed into himself, unable to take any more." Decades earlier director Peter Bogdanovich visited with Dean in his dressing room on the MGM lot to talk about acting: "I kinda think back to somethin' that's happened to me. Like in *Rio Bravo*, there was a scene I was supposed to be very sad in, supposed to cry even. So I thought about a time I was unhappy, a time when my son, little Dino, was very sick and that helped me." Not so impervious as we might think, Dino's thick carapace had been pierced straight through to the heart.

Jerry Lewis had come to Dean Paul's funeral, stood quietly in the back of the church and then left to return to Las Vegas. Later that night upon learning of his old partner's presence, Dino retreated to his den, and the two spoke privately on the telephone for over a half an hour.

Dino holds son Dean Paul, Jeanne looks on

When he emerged, he said, "I just thanked him." Jerry in his book recounts that conversation: "All he kept saying was, 'Jer, I can't tell you.'" They remained friends for the rest of Martin's life.

Famous reunion between Dean and Jerry arranged by Frank Sinatra, 1976.
The pair had not talked for twenty years.
A surprised Lewis called it one of the most memorable moments of his career

Broken but stoic, Dino endured. He performed rarely then quit altogether. Most of those close to him believe that after the tragic loss of his son, he "closed up on life." But Jerry and Jeanne, the two who loved him best were back; he talked to his former partner regularly, and he lived five blocks away from his former wife. He had the rest of his children who were devoted to him; the family had dinner at Jeanne's on Sunday nights. But things were not as they had been, decades of smoking had ravaged his lungs. And there was no denying the atmosphere of sadness around the dying old man. And boredom. His son Ricci Martin felt, "His heart just wasn't in it anymore." He who mastered the art of letting go, had nothing more to hold onto when the death of his son loosened his last grip on life. He retreated further into his solitude. Some say it was a dark ending, but maybe he felt more free; there was nothing more he had to do. He kept his privacy and his dignity. In the end, he quit eating; he wanted to go, and so, just like his mother, Dino died on Christmas morning. I like to think he went gracefully with courage as he lived, in his own way. I'd like to think, I want to think, his end wasn't so bad—he was still Dino, our beloved Dino.

Jeanne expected it, but Jerry, playing the devil in *Damn Yankees*, was "completely shattered and grief-stricken." He immediately flew out to LA. Dino had asked that there be no tears at his funeral; true to his nature, he wanted everyone to have a good time—he knew he'd had a good run. Frank Sinatra was too distraught to attend; Rosemary Clooney sang a slowed down, sad version of

Everybody Loves Somebody Sometime; Shirley MacLaine quipped, "Well, I just talked to Dean, about an hour ago." Jerry delivered the eulogy; defying Jeanne's request to keep it light, his expressive love made many cry including himself.

Dino was buried in his best tux. On the occasion of what would have been his 90th birthday, I, like a devotee visiting a shrine, drive to the Westwood Memorial Park, an urban cemetery located one block south and east of Wilshire and Westwood, which is one of the busiest corners in LA. But I can't find it amid the huge high rises and parking structures. Desperate, I go into a Rite-Aid pharmacy for help where a clerk instructs me to walk down an alley between the buildings. And finally, there it is in the middle of the city, an expanse of green with gray stones carved with the names of the dead. There are different sections of vaults named the Sanctuary of Love, of Devotion, of Tranquillity, of Remembrance, of Tenderness, of Peace. Shades of *The Loved One*! All I need now is for the embalmer Mr. Joyboy to bounce by.

Dino's crypt is in the Sanctuary of Love, three rows above the ground. His bronze plaque is engraved with his name, the dates of the span of his life, and the epitaph, *Everybody Loves Somebody Sometime*. Some tourist stands next to me; I am not a tourist but a pilgrim. I am not here scouting out celebrity grave sites, I am in love. The Park is a popular favorite with stars since Marilyn Monroe (who died while making a film with Dino) was buried here.

Today, a huge heart-shaped bouquet rests against her stone. Just south from Dino is Billy Wilder, whose tombstone reads:

> I'm A Writer
> But Then
> Nobody's Perfect

I put my flowers next to the fresh roses already in the vase attached to his vault; I wait out the tourist. Alone at last, I have wild fantasies about running into Dino's family and bowing before them. Then I calm down.

Pennies, nickels, dimes, quarters line the top lip of his plaque, some old Italian tradition? *Everybody Loves Somebody Sometime*, he exhorts us to love. I stand before his grave; I thank him for his life and the work, tell him he is the modern Falstaff. What to say? What can my words do for him in death? Yet I thank him again for the delight he has brought to me and to millions of others, still, to this very day. But he doesn't need me or my praise; I need him—his way of ease, of being free. Sometimes before the dead, the living ask for favors. I put my hands over his name and ask for help: "Let me feel free. May I escape from the savage attacks of the persecutor within." Standing in a shaft of light in the otherwise gloomy Sanctuary of Love, I wonder, is this all right?

Then a white delivery trunk pulls up, *Matsumoto and Sons*, written on its side. A boy carrying a huge bouquet of red roses appears. I ask if they are for Dean. He nods and places them down below the plaque. When he leaves, I can't help myself—I rip open the small white envelope. It says:

> Happy Birthday Dean
> Loving you always,
> Francis

The Man! The Chairman of the Board! Francis Sinatra! Is it something in his will, on Dean's birthday in perpetuity, always send him flowers? I am not alone in my worship today. I feel the thrill of connection–I'm on the bus, in the inner sanctum of vibes, here by right of my affinity! Then I am struck by how we mere mortals want to assert that our love is forever, the immortality of our love.

How often we hear the phrase, how it's important, "to be free." It's in our blood as Americans, "the freest country in the world." Whether it's part of our national heritage or just the plain longing of any human being, I know I yearn for it. Often, mostly, I don't feel free but trapped by social conditions and internal voices of criticism. And yet, and yet, there rises up that renewing spark: Life is for me! What if we turn to models of freedom and courage because yes, it takes courage to be free, to stand outside cultural assumptions and to discover the ground of your own personality. I noticed such models of freedom towards whom a natural affinity flowed. The archetypal principle of freedom is the Fool, an ancient mystical symbol and an actual social role at its height in Medieval and Renaissance times. And from that universal image came to me through the particulars of space and time, two people, one a literary star, one a Hollywood star, Falstaff and Dino–irresistible and subversive.

There are many outer and inner structures that mean us no good. The power of the machine of the state is on the rise, and individual freedom, true freedom does not exist in parroted patriotic slogans but, rather, in the ability to find one's own voice, the greatest treasure imaginable. Many of us seek release from controlling forces. I turned to Falstaff, then Dino. Writer Anthony Burgess thought that "The Falstaffian spirit is a great sustainer of civilization. It disappears when the state is too powerful and when people worry too much about their souls." The state condemns us, and we condemn ourselves. But not for our two lads a repressive sense of duty and crippling guilt. Oh no, Falstaff questions every code of conduct and with great integrity makes his own way. Dino bravely faces the audience and follows his bliss at every opportunity. What makes them free is their own minds, the independence of their inner thoughts regardless of the outer circumstances.

Ironically, both men are often regarded as figures of anarchy, opposed to the necessary order of civilization. In the Tarot cards, the essence of the Fool is thought to be like Burgess's Falstaffian spirit, a basis of civilization, creative energy as the foundation of cultural power. And contrary to what we might have learned in fifth grade, this spirit of freedom allows for the play of the imagination, the greatest force for evolution.

Maybe we wouldn't want all the laws of England at mercurial Falstaff's command, but he is preferable to Henry; at least we wouldn't be fighting and dying in useless wars. Who has caused more suffering, Falstaff or the Henrys—father and son?

And carefree Dino may be unreliable in mundane matters, I wouldn't ask him for a ride to the airport or expect him to discipline his children. Nor would I ask Falstaff to hold my purse for me. With their irregular habits, they certainly don't function as normal members of society partly because they refuse to accept predigested codes of behavior not in their own best interests. But there is no denying that it is so much fun to be in their company, that their very presence brings relief from the tensions of the ordinary world and bestows upon us the magical spirit of play. We need autonomy, freedom from external control and internalized conditioning. Falstaff has fascinated humanity for centuries, the Fool for millennia, Dino since the mid-twentieth century. We turn to them because they manifest what Renaissance essayist Michel de Montaigne calls, "The most certain sign of wisdom...cheerfulness."

Falstaff and Dino share a comic vision of life and are willing to risk being fools. Falstaff possesses a character of great vitality and no malice. I feel like I could never exhaust my study of him. As Herschel Baker perceives: "Falstaff's energizing wit endows us with a fresh awareness." Once in a dream, the professor who introduced me to Shakespeare tells me, "Falstaff holds all the secrets of life." Dino too had many complex facets to his personality. Jerry recounts Dino's supreme confidence: "Dean had this uncanny way of making everything bad look like it wasn't all *that* bad."

Director Cameron Crowe in his late conversations with Billy Wilder asked the aging filmmaker about Dean. Billy loved him: "Dino was a first-class guy, a first-class talent...But there was much more, 90 per cent more to him than just the jokester. Yeah, I am a sucker for Dean Martin. I thought he was the funniest man in Hollywood." Crowe also mentioned that Martin Scorsese was planning a film biography of Dean Martin. Where is *that* picture? People

Billy and Dino share a laugh

from all classes of society loved Dino and made him a star. Through contact with the public, his son realized: "It wasn't only the famous who loved Dad...It was also regular men and women who cherished him...who appreciated his unassuming style and sense of fun." Apparently Dino, (who loved comic books), had a favorite cartoon that he kept in his various dressing rooms. Two discontented office workers trapped in their jobs, one says to the other, "When I die, I want to come back as Dean Martin."

But as we know, their Fool's wisdom did not carry them to the end. We may be more familiar with our suffering than with our sense of freedom. Many times in our lives, we die to what we thought we were, fixed identities fall apart, we lose our dreams, lovers depart. All we can do is turn to the quintessence of the Fool in hopes of renewal.

Again and again the Fool falls off the cliff, choosing to start something new, choosing yet another adventure. Falstaff and Dino lived by the dictates of their own hearts, free to love and free to have their hearts broken. If they carried their grief till their ends, I hope that the joy they have given me is with me till my end in one shape or another. The Fool's energy is eternal, the ever renewing Life Force; nothing is more important than this. This is the best resting place of the imagination. To counter the million sounds of no! in our worlds, the breath of one more yes. All we need is one more yes.

Illustration Sources

Prologue

Falstaff

16 "Henry of Bolingbroke, flanked by the lords spiritual and temporal, claims the throne in 1399". From a contemporary manuscript, British Library, Harley 1319,f.57. *Wikimedia Commons/Public Domain.*

17 *Falstaff with big wine jar and cup* by Eduard von Grützner, 1896. *Wikimedia Commons/Public Domain.*

19 Falstaff plays Prince Hal, etched by George Cruikshank for *The Life of Sir John Falstaff*, 1858. *Public Domain.*

21 The better part of valor, etched by George Cruikshank for *The Life of Sir John Falstaff*, 1858. *Public Domain.*

22 Samuel Phelps and Sadler's Wells Theater, illustration, author unknown, 1845. *Public Domain.*

22 Henry Beerbohm Tree, photogravure, 1896. *Public Domain.*

22 JH Hackett, 1850. Public *Domain.*

23 Roger Allam as Falstaff in *Henry IV Part 1*, directed by Dominic Dromgoole, 2010. *Geraint Lewis / Alamy.*

24 Achilles killing a Trojan prisoner in front of Charun, side A from an Etruscan red-figure calyx-crater, end of the 4th century BCE. *Wikimedia Commons/Public Domain.*

24 The death of Hotspur illustrated in *A Chronicle of England: B.C. 55 – A.D. 1485* by James William Edmund Doyle, 1864. *Wikimedia Commons/Public Domain.*

25 *Falstaff Carrying Dead Hotspur* by Henry William Bunbury, watercolor, pen and black ink, late 18th century. *Yale Center for British Art, Paul Mellon Fund, Public Domain.*

26 *3:10* to Yuma, poster. *Wikimedia Commons/Public Domain Under Fair Use.*

27 Kirk Douglas Theater. *Wikimedia Commons/Public Domain.*

28 Harry Potter poster. *Wikimedia Commons/Public Domain, Creative Commons Attribution Share Alike.*

29 Antony Sher as Falstaff, A Royal Shakespeare Company Production directed by Gregory Doran, 2014. *Geraint Lewis / Alamy.*

30 *King Henry V at the Battle of Agincourt* by John Gilbert, 1884. *Wikimedia Commons/Public Domain.*

31 Joan of Arc depicted on horseback in an illustration from a 1505 manuscript. *Wikimedia Commons/Public Domain.*

33 Orson Welles as Falstaff in *Chimes at Midnight*, 1965. *AF archive / Alamy.*

The Fool

Page

36 The Fool Tarot card from the Rider-Waite-Smith deck, drawn by Pamela Coleman Smith, 1909. *Wikimedia Commons/Public Domain.*

38 *Foolishness* by Giotto, fresco, 1306, Padua, Italy. This depiction resembles the Fool in the earliest surviving painted decks. *Wikimedia Commons/Public Domain.*

38 The Fool card from the Visconti-Sforza Tarot deck (*Tarocchi dei Visconti*), 1450. The Fool depicted as a ragged vagabond. *Wikimedia Commons/Public Domain.*

38 Joker card from modern deck. *Wikimedia Commons/Public Domain.*

40 The World Tarot card from the Rider-Waite-Smith deck, drawn by Pamela Coleman Smith, 1909. *Wikimedia Commons/Public Domain.*

41 Bellows. *Wikimedia Commons/Public Domain.*

42 Xochi and Marka Maberry Gaulke. *Courtesy of Sue Maberry.*

43 Will Sommers court jester to Henry VIII, engraving by Francis Delaram c. 1615–24. *Wikimedia Commons/Public Domain.*

44   Henry VIII with his jester and his children, early 1550s. *Wikimedia Commons/Public Domain.*

44   *A Court Fool*, Facsimile of a Woodcut in the "Cosmographie Universelle" of Munster: folio (Basle, 1552). *Eon Images.*

45   *Portrait of Archibald Armstrong*, "Archee the kinges lester," by Thomas Cecill, circa 1630-1640. *Wikimedia Commons/Public Domain.*

46   *Raja Birbal,*16th century wit, painting by unknown Mughal artist in 19th century. *Wikimedia Commons/Public Domain.*

46   *Buffoon playing a Lute* painting by Frans Hals, circa 1623. *Wikimedia Commons/Public Domain.*

46   A 14th-century miniature representing the Feast of Fools. *Wikimedia Commons/Public Domain.*

47   *The Lord of Misrule*, illustration from Cassell's *Illustrated History of England*, 19th century. *Wikimedia Commons/Public Domain.*

48   The tomb of Dicky Pierce, Church of St.Mary in Berkeley village, 1728. *Courtesy of cotswold.info.* His epitaph by Jonathan Swift reads:
> Here lies the Earl of Suffolk's fool,
> Men call him Dicky Pearce;
> His folly serv'd to make men laugh
> When wit and mirth were scarce.
>
> Poor Dick, alas! is dead and gone,
> What signifies to cry?
> Dickies enough he left behind
> To laugh at by-and-by.

48   Calendar, *Wikimedia Commons/Public Domain.*

49   Maynard G. Krebs. *Wikimedia Commons/Public Domain.*

49   Gore Vidal, portrait by Carl Van Vechten, 1948. *Wikimedia Commons/Public Domain.*

80   Dean Martin with wife Jeanne, 1954. *ZUMA Press, Inc. / Alamy.*

81   *The Young Lions*, 1958. *Photos 12 / Alamy.*

82   *Some Came Running*, 1958. *INTERFOTO / Alamy.*

83   *Rio Bravo*, 1959. *Wikimedia Commons/Public Domain.*

84   Poster for film *Who was that Lady?*, 1960. *Wikimedia Commons/ Public Domain.*

85   Hand and footprints at the Grauman's Chinese Theater. *Wikimedia Commons/Public Domain.*

85   Dean with his family at Grauman's Chinese Theater. *Photos 12 / Alamy.*

86   *Bells Are Ringing*, 1960. *Pictorial Press Ltd / Alamy.*

86   *Ocean's 11*,1960. *Wikimedia Commons/Public Domain.*

87   Dean and Shirley MacLaine, *Ocean's 11*, 1960. *AF archive / Alamy.*

88   The Sands Sign. *Wikimedia Commons/Public Domain.*

88   The Rat Pack performing: Frank Sinatra, Sammy Davis Jr., Dean Martin, Peter Lawford and Joey Bishop. *ImageCollect.com/Bill Kobrin/Globe Photos, Inc.*

89   Publicity photo of Dean Martin and Frank Sinatra, January 30, 1958. *Wikimedia Commons/Public Domain.*

89   Frank Sinatra with Dean Martin at Celebrity Golf in Los Angeles. *ImageCollect.com/ Phil Roach/Globe Photos, Inc.*

91   On the set of *Kiss Me, Stupid,* 1964. *ImageCollect.com/ Winson Muldrow/Globe Photos, Inc.*

92   Dean Martin on location with Kim Novak. *ImageCollect.com/ Winson Muldrow/Globe Photos, Inc.*

93   *The Dean Martin Show*, 1966. *Courtesy of dinopaulcrocetti. tumblr.*

111 *Falstaff at the Boar's Head Tavern* by Edward Grutzner, 1909. *Wikimedia Commons/Public Domain.*

112 The Peasants' Feast, from "The Twelve Months" engraving by Hans Beham, 1546. *Wikimedia Commons/Public Domain.*

113 Justice Swallow tries to get Falstaff to stay for the night illustrated by H. C. Selous, 1830. *Wikimedia Commons/Public Domain.*

113 Pistol informing Sir John Falstaff of the Death of Henry the fourth etched by George Cruikshank for *The Life of Sir John Falstaff,* 1858. *Public Domain.*

115 Sir John Falstaff receiving a most unexpected rebuke from King Henry the fifth, etched by George Cruikshank for *The Life of Sir John Falstaff,* 1858. *Public Domain.*

116 Gower Memorial of Prince Hal at Stratford-upon-Avon. *Courtesy of Immanuel Giel released to Wikimedia Commons*

116 Gower Memorial of Falstaff at Stratford-upon-Avon. *Photo: Colourbox.com.*

117 Last scene in the life of Falstaff etched by George Cruikshank for *The Life of Sir John Falstaff,* 1858. *Public Domain.*

119 Dean Paul Martin playing tennis. *Ronald Grant Archive / Alamy.*

121 Jeanne and Dean Martin with their son Dean Paul Martin. *ZUMA Press, Inc. / Alamy.*

121 Frank Sinatra with Dean Martin and Jerry Lewis, at the Muscular Dystrophy Association Labor Day telethon, 1976. *Wikimedia Commons/Public Domain.*

124 Dean's crypt. *Photograph by Starr Goode.*

125 Frank's flowers. *Photograph by Starr Goode.*

129 Billy Wilder and Dean Martin. *Courtesy of They Were Collaborators.*

About the Author

Starr Goode, MA, teaches literature at Santa Monica College. Producer and moderator for the cable TV series, *The Goddess in Art*, it is now available on YouTube. She has been profiled for her work as a cultural commentator in the *LA Weekly*, the *Los Angeles Times*, the *Wall Street Journal*, and *The New Yorker*. Her new book, *Sheela na gig, The Dark Goddess of Sacred Power*, will be published in the fall of 2016 by Inner Traditions.